The magnificent primitive drama no people can ever live again!

First published forty years ago, *Black Elk Speaks* is one of the greatest of all books about the life of the American Indian.

A book of legend, a book of personal vision that makes the LSD trip seem pale by comparison, this is also the story of a people now almost totally destroyed, of their life on this planet and their harmony with the forces of nature, and of Black Elk himself—warrior and medicine man—born at the end of an era . . . and destined to watch it fade.

"A unique, realistic, and poetic understanding of a vanished time and people."
—*Oliver La Farge*

Books by John G. Neihardt

Black Elk Speaks
When the Tree Flowered

Publishd by POCKET BOOKS

BLACK ELK SPEAKS

*Being the Life Story of a Holy
Man of the Oglala Sioux*

as told through
JOHN G. NEIHARDT
(Flaming Rainbow)

Illustrated by
STANDING BEAR

PUBLISHED BY POCKET BOOKS NEW YORK

The text of the Bison Book edition of *Black Elk Speaks* was reproduced from the 1932 edition published by William Morrow & Company. The original title read "as told to" John G. Neihardt. The change to the form now appearing on the title page was made at the author's rquest.

The spelling "Ogalala" occurs on pages 51, 79, 94, and elsewhere throughout the text. The spelling now preferred is "Oglala."

 POCKET BOOKS, a Simon & Schuster division of
GULF & WESTERN CORPORATION
1230 Avenue of the Americas, New York, N.Y. 10020

Copyright 1932, © 1959 by John G. Neihardt

Library of Congress Catalog Card Number: 61-7236

ISBN: 0-671-82144-X

First Pocket Books printing April, 1972

16 15 14 13

POCKET and colophon are trademarks of Simon & Schuster.

Printed in the U.S.A.

The paintings following page 110 are by Standing Bear, the artist of the Oglala Sioux. The publishers wish to acknowledge the courtesy of John G. Neihardt and the Western Historical Manuscripts Collection of the University of Missouri at Columbia, for permission to reproduce them here.

WHAT IS GOOD IN THIS BOOK
IS GIVEN BACK
TO THE SIX GRANDFATHERS
AND
TO THE GREAT MEN OF MY PEOPLE

—BLACK ELK.

Preface

The Book That Would Not Die

It was during August, 1930, that I first met Black Elk. I was then working on *The Song of the Messiah,* which now stands as the fifth and final narrative poem in my *Cycle of the West.* This *Song* is concerned with what white men have called the "Messiah craze"—the great Messianic dream that came to the desperate Indians in the middle 80's of the 19th century and ended with the massacre at Wounded Knee, South Dakota, on December 29, 1890.

With my son, Sigurd, I had gone to Pine Ridge Reservation for the purpose of finding some old medicine man who had been active in the Messiah Movement and who might somehow be induced to talk to me about the deeper spiritual significance of the matter. I had known many of the Oglala Sioux for some years, and had good friends among the old "long-hairs." It was not information that was lacking for my purpose. I had the facts, both from the records and from old men who had lived through that time, sharing the great hope and the tragic disillusionment. What I needed for my purpose was something to be experienced through intimate contact,

rather than to be received through telling. (Those of my readers who may be familiar with my *Song of the Messiah* will know what is meant.)

Through the Field Agent-in-Charge at Pine Ridge Agency I learned of an old Sioux by the name of Black Elk, who lived among the barren hills some twenty miles east of the Agency near Manderson post office. Black Elk was a "kind of preacher," I was told—that is to say, a *wichasha wakon* (holy man, priest)—and he had been of some importance in the Messiah affair. Also, he was second cousin to Crazy Horse, the principal hero of my *Song of the Indian Wars,* and had known the great chieftain well.

So my son and I drove over to Manderson to try our luck with the old man. Flying Hawk, an interpreter with whom I was slightly acquainted, was living there, and he was willing to go with us to see Black Elk at his home about four miles west of Manderson. It was a dead-end road that led through the treeless, yellow hills to Black Elk's home—a one-room log cabin with weeds growing out of the dirt roof.

When we arrived, Black Elk was standing outside a shelter made of pine boughs. It was noon. When we left, after sunset, Flying Hawk said, "That was kind of funny, the way the old man seemed to know you were coming!" My son remarked that he had the same impression; and when I had known the great old man for some years I was quite prepared to believe that he did know, for he certainly had supernatural powers.

Shaking hands with Black Elk, I told him that I was well acquainted with the Omaha Indians and with many of the Sioux, that I had come to get acquainted with him and have a little talk about old

times. "Ah-h-h!" he said, indicating that my suggestion was satisfactory.

For some time, Black Elk, with his near-blind stare fixed on the ground, seemed to have forgotten us. I was about to break the silence by way of getting something started, when the old man looked up to Flying Hawk, the interpreter, and said (speaking Sioux, for he knew no English): "As I sit here, I can feel in this man beside me a strong desire to know the things of the Other World. He has been sent to learn what I know, and I will teach him."

Finally, the old man began talking about a vision that had come to him in his youth. It was his power-vision, as I learned later, and his fragmentary references to it were evidently intended only to arouse my curiosity, for he could not speak freely about a matter so sacred before the assembled company. It was like half seeing, half sensing a strange and beautiful landscape by brief flashes of sheet lightning.

Often I broke the old man's prolonged silences by referring to the old times before the evil days began and the white men possessed the land. I recalled great battles, high moments in Sioux history, and he would respond politely; but it was increasingly clear that his real interest was in "the things of the Other World."

The sun was near to setting when Black Elk said: "There is so much to teach you. What I know was given to me for men and it is true and it is beautiful. Soon I shall be under the grass and it will be lost. You were sent to save it, and you must come back so that I can teach you." And I said: "I will come back, Black Elk. When do you want me?" He replied, "In the spring when the grass is so high," indicating the breadth of a hand.

That winter I corresponded with Black Elk through his son, Ben, who had attended Carlisle for a year or two, and thus arrangements were made for an extended visit the following spring.

During early May, 1931, in company with my eldest daughter, Enid, who had been my secretary for several years, and my second daughter, Hilda, I returned to Black Elk's home so that he might relate his life story to me in fulfillment of a duty that he felt incumbent upon him. His chief purpose was to "save his Great Vision for men."

It was my function to translate the old man's story, not only in the factual sense—for it was not the facts that mattered most—but rather to re-create in English the mood and manner of the old man's narrative. This was often a grueling and difficult task, requiring much patient effort and careful questioning of the interpreter.

Always I felt it a sacred obligation to be true to the old man's meaning and manner of expression. I am convinced there were times when we had more than the ordinary means of communication.

For the last forty years it has been my purpose to bring Black Elk's message to the white world as he wished me to do. This book has had, and is still having a remarkable career. First printed in 1932, it received an enthusiastic reception from literary critics who regarded it as a strangely beautiful book, although they had little knowledge of Indians.

The general public, with practically no knowledge of Indians, gave it a very modest reception. In less than two years the publisher "remaindered" the edition at forty-five cents a copy and the book was forgotten.

A generation passed, but the book refused to die.

PREFACE

Somehow a copy found its way to Zurich, Switzerland and was appreciated by a group of German scholars, including the late Carl Jung, the famous psychologist and philosopher.

The news of the book reached America and found some friendly appreciators. Copies were obtainable only in rare book stores and sold at premium prices.

In 1961, *Black Elk Speaks* was reissued in paperback and was enthusiastically received, particularly among young people. In the words of the *Christian Herald,* it became "the current youth classic." In 1971, as a result of Dick Cavett's television interview with the author, the book exploded into surprising popularity.

Black Elk Speaks' fame is spreading throughout the United States and also in Europe, having been translated into eight languages.

The old prophet's wish that I bring his message to the world is actually being fulfilled.

Those who are acquainted with *Black Elk Speaks* will remember the old man's prayer on Harney Peak when he wept in the drizzling rain and cried out in desperation to the Grandfathers of the Universe: "A pitiful old man you see me here, and I have fallen away and have done nothing."

Perhaps with his message spreading across the world he has not failed.

John G. Neihardt
Columbia, Missouri
November, 1971

Contents

	PREFACE	ix
I.	THE OFFERING OF THE PIPE	1
II.	EARLY BOYHOOD	6
III.	THE GREAT VISION	17
IV.	THE BISON HUNT	40
V.	AT THE SOLDIERS' TOWN	51
VI.	HIGH HORSE'S COURTING	56
VII.	WASICHUS IN THE HILLS	64
VIII.	THE FIGHT WITH THREE STARS	77
IX.	THE RUBBING OUT OF LONG HAIR	88
X.	WALKING THE BLACK ROAD	110
XI.	THE KILLING OF CRAZY HORSE	118
XII.	GRANDMOTHER'S LAND	123
XIII.	THE COMPELLING FEAR	131
XIV.	THE HORSE DANCE	136
XV.	THE DOG VISION	149
XVI.	HEYOKA CEREMONY	159
XVII.	THE FIRST CURE	164
XVIII.	THE POWERS OF THE BISON AND THE ELK	173
XIX.	ACROSS THE BIG WATER	181

Contents

XX.	THE SPIRIT JOURNEY	190
XXI.	THE MESSIAH	195
XXII.	VISIONS OF THE OTHER WORLD	203
XXIII.	BAD TROUBLE COMING	211
XXIV.	THE BUTCHERING AT WOUNDED KNEE	217
XXV.	THE END OF THE DREAM	224
	AUTHOR'S POSTSCRIPT	231
	ABOUT THIS BOOK AND ITS AUTHOR	235

Original illustrations appear between pages 110-111

BLACK ELK SPEAKS

I

The Offering of the Pipe

Black Elk Speaks:
My friend, I am going to tell you the story of my life, as you wish; and if it were only the story of my life I think I would not tell it; for what is one man that he should make much of his winters, even when they bend him like a heavy snow? So many other men have lived and shall live that story, to be grass upon the hills.

It is the story of all life that is holy and is good to tell, and of us two-leggeds sharing in it with the four-leggeds and the wings of the air and all green things; for these are children of one mother and their father is one Spirit.

This, then, is not the tale of a great hunter or of a great warrior, or of a great traveler, although I have made much meat in my time and fought for my people both as boy and man, and have gone far and seen strange lands and men. So also have many others done, and better than I. These things I shall remember by the way, and often they may seem to be the very tale itself, as when I was living them in happiness and sorrow. But now that I can see it all as from a lonely hilltop, I know it was the story of a

mighty vision given to a man too weak to use it; of a holy tree that should have flourished in a people's heart with flowers and singing birds, and now is withered; and of a people's dream that died in bloody snow.

But if the vision was true and mighty, as I know, it is true and mighty yet; for such things are of the spirit, and it is in the darkness of their eyes that men get lost.

So I know that it is a good thing I am going to do; and because no good thing can be done by any man alone, I will first make an offering and send a voice to the Spirit of the World, that it may help me to be true. See, I fill this sacred pipe with the bark of the red willow; but before we smoke it, you must see how it is made and what it means. These four ribbons hanging here on the stem are the four quarters of the universe. The black one is for the west where the thunder beings live to send us rain; the white one for the north, whence comes the great white cleansing wind; the red one for the east, whence springs the light and where the morning star lives to give men wisdom; the yellow for the south, whence come the summer and the power to grow.

But these four spirits are only one Spirit after all, and this eagle feather here is for that One, which is like a father, and also it is for the thoughts of men that should rise high as eagles do. Is not the sky a father and the earth a mother, and are not all living things with feet or wings or roots their children? And this hide upon the mouthpiece here, which should be bison hide, is for the earth, from whence we came and at whose breast we suck as babies all our lives, along with all the animals and birds and trees and

grasses. And because it means all this, and more than any man can understand, the pipe is holy.

There is a story about the way the pipe first came to us. A very long time ago, they say, two scouts were out looking for bison; and when they came to the top of a high hill and looked north, they saw something coming a long way off, and when it came closer they cried out, "It is a woman!," and it was. Then one of the scouts, being foolish, had bad thoughts and spoke them; but the other said: "That is a sacred woman; throw all bad thoughts away." When she came still closer, they saw that she wore a fine white buckskin dress, that her hair was very long and that she was young and very beautiful. And she knew their thoughts and said in a voice that was like singing: "You do not know me, but if you want to do as you think, you may come." And the foolish one went; but just as he stood before her, there was a white cloud that came and covered them. And the beautiful young woman came out of the cloud, and when it blew away the foolish man was a skeleton covered with worms.

Then the woman spoke to the one who was not foolish: "You shall go home and tell your people that I am coming and that a big tepee shall be built for me in the center of the nation." And the man, who was very much afraid, went quickly and told the people, who did at once as they were told; and there around the big tepee they waited for the sacred woman. And after a while she came, very beautiful and singing, and as she went into the tepee this is what she sang:

"With visible breath I am walking.
A voice I am sending as I walk.

In a sacred manner I am walking.
With visible tracks I am walking.
In a sacred manner I walk."

And as she sang, there came from her mouth a white
cloud that was good to smell. Then she gave some-
thing to the chief, and it was a pipe with a bison
calf carved on one side to mean the earth that bears
and feeds us, and with twelve eagle feathers hanging
from the stem to mean the sky and the twelve
moons, and these were tied with a grass that never
breaks. "Behold!" she said. "With this you shall
multiply and be a good nation. Nothing but good
shall come from it. Only the hands of the good shall
take care of it and the bad shall not even see it."
Then she sang again and went out of the tepee; and
as the people watched her going, suddenly it was a
white bison galloping away and snorting, and soon
it was gone.

This they tell, and whether it happened so or not
I do not know; but if you think about it, you can see
that it is true.

Now I light the pipe, and after I have offered it
to the powers that are one Power, and sent forth a
voice to them, we shall smoke together. Offering
the mouthpiece first of all to the One above—so—
I send a voice:

Hey hey! hey hey! hey hey! hey hey!

Grandfather, Great Spirit, you have been always,
and before you no one has been. There is no other
one to pray to but you. You yourself, everything
that you see, everything has been made by you. The
star nations all over the universe you have finished.
The four quarters of the earth you have finished.
The day, and in that day, everything you have fin-

ished. Grandfather, Great Spirit, lean close to the earth that you may hear the voice I send. You towards where the sun goes down, behold me; Thunder Beings, behold me! You where the White Giant lives in power, behold me! You where the sun shines continually, whence come the day-break star and the day, behold me! You where the summer lives, behold me! You in the depths of the heavens, an eagle of power, behold! And you, Mother Earth, the only Mother, you who have shown mercy to your children!

Hear me, four quarters of the world—a relative I am! Give me the strength to walk the soft earth, a relative to all that is! Give me the eyes to see and the strength to understand, that I may be like you. With your power only can I face the winds.

Great Spirit, Great Spirit, my Grandfather, all over the earth the faces of living things are all alike. With tenderness have these come up out of the ground. Look upon these faces of children without number and with children in their arms, that they may face the winds and walk the good road to the day of quiet.

This is my prayer; hear me! The voice I have sent is weak, yet with earnestness I have sent it. Hear me!

It is finished. Hetchetu aloh!

Now, my friend, let us smoke together so that there may be only good between us.

II

Early Boyhood

I am a Lakota of the Ogalala band. My father's
name was Black Elk, and his father before him bore
the name, and the father of his father, so that I am
the fourth to bear it. He was a medicine man and so
were several of his brothers. Also, he and the great
Crazy Horse's father were cousins, having the same
grandfather. My mother's name was White Cow
Sees; her father was called Refuse-to-go, and her
mother, Plenty Eagle Feathers. I can remember my
mother's mother and her father. My father's father
was killed by the Pawnees when I was too little to
know, and his mother, Red Eagle Woman, died soon
after.

I was born in the Moon of the Popping Trees
(December) on the Little Powder River in the Win-
ter When the Four Crows Were Killed (1863), and
I was three years old when my father's right leg was
broken in the Battle of the Hundred Slain.[1] From
that wound he limped until the day he died, which

[1] The Fetterman Fight, commonly described as a "mas-
sacre," in which Captain Fetterman and 81 men were wiped
out on Peno Creek near Fort Phil Kearney, December 21,
1866.

was about the time when Big Foot's band was butchered on Wounded Knee (1890). He is buried here in these hills.

I can remember that Winter of the Hundred Slain as a man may remember some bad dream he dreamed when he was little, but I can not tell just how much I heard when I was bigger and how much I understood when I was little. It is like some fearful thing in a fog, for it was a time when everything seemed troubled and afraid.

I had never seen a Wasichu[2] then, and did not know what one looked like; but every one was saying that the Wasichus were coming and that they were going to take our country and rub us all out and that we should all have to die fighting. It was the Wasichus who got rubbed out in that battle, and all the people were talking about it for a long while; but a hundred Wasichus was not much if there were others and others without number where those came from.

I remember once that I asked my grandfather about this. I said: "When the scouts come back from seeing the prairie full of bison somewhere, the people say the Wasichus are coming; and when strange men are coming to kill us all, they say the Wasichus are coming. What does it mean?" And he said, "That they are many."

When I was older, I learned what the fighting was about that winter and the next summer. Up on the Madison Fork the Wasichus had found much of the yellow metal that they worship and that makes them crazy, and they wanted to have a road up through

[2] A term used to designate the white man, but having no reference to the color of his skin.

our country to the place where the yellow metal was; but my people did not want the road. It would scare the bison and make them go away, and also it would let the other Wasichus come in like a river. They told us that they wanted only to use a little land, as much as a wagon would take between the wheels; but our people knew better. And when you look about you now, you can see what it was they wanted.

Once we were happy in our own country and we were seldom hungry, for then the two-leggeds and the four-leggeds lived together like relatives, and there was plenty for them and for us. But the Wasichus came, and they have made little islands for us and other little islands for the four-leggeds, and always these islands are becoming smaller, for around them surges the gnawing flood of the Wasichu; and it is dirty with lies and greed.

A long time ago my father told me what his father told him, that there was once a Lakota holy man, called Drinks Water, who dreamed what was to be; and this was long before the coming of the Wasichus. He dreamed that the four-leggeds were going back into the earth and that a strange race had woven a spider's web all around the Lakotas. And he said: "When this happens, you shall live in square gray houses, in a barren land, and beside those square gray houses you shall starve." They say he went back to Mother Earth soon after he saw this vision, and it was sorrow that killed him. You can look about you now and see that he meant these dirt-roofed houses we are living in, and that all the rest was true. Sometimes dreams are wiser than waking.

And so when the soldiers came and built them-

selves a town of logs there on the Piney Fork of the Powder, my people knew they meant to have their road and take our country and maybe kill us all when they were strong enough. Crazy Horse was only about 19 years old then, and Red Cloud was still our great chief. In the Moon of the Changing Season (October) he called together all the scattered bands of the Lakota for a big council on the Powder River, and when we went on the warpath against the soldiers, a horseback could ride through our villages from sunrise until the day was above his head, so far did our camp stretch along the valley of the river; for many of our friends, the Shyela[3] and the Blue Clouds,[4] had come to help us fight.

And it was about when the bitten moon was delayed (last quarter) in the Time of the Popping Trees when the hundred were rubbed out. My friend, Fire Thunder here, who is older than I, was in that fight and he can tell you how it was.

Fire Thunder Speaks:

I was 16 years old when this happened, and after the big council on the Powder we had moved over to the Tongue River where we were camping at the mouth of Peno Creek. There were many of us there. Red Cloud was over all of us, but the chief of our band was Big Road. We started out on horseback just about sunrise, riding up the creek toward the soldiers' town on the Piney, for we were going to attack it. The sun was about half way up when we stopped at the place where the Wasichu's road came down a steep, narrow ridge and crossed the creek.

[3] Cheyennes.
[4] Arapahoes.

It was a good place to fight, so we sent some men ahead to coax the soldiers out. While they were gone, we divided into two parts and hid in the gullies on both sides of the ridge and waited. After a long while we heard a shot up over the hill, and we knew the soldiers were coming. So we held the noses of our ponies that they might not whinny at the soldiers' horses. Soon we saw our men coming back, and some of them were walking and leading their horses, so that the soldiers would think they were worn out. Then the men we had sent ahead came running down the road between us, and the soldiers on horseback followed, shooting. When they came to the flat at the bottom of the hill, the fighting began all at once. I had a sorrel horse, and just as I was going to get on him, the soldiers turned around and began to fight their way back up the hill. I had a six-shooter that I had traded for, and also a bow and arrows. When the soldiers started back, I held my sorrel with one hand and began killing them with the six-shooter, for they came close to me. There were many bullets, but there were more arrows—so many that it was like a cloud of grasshoppers all above and around the soldiers; and our people, shooting across, hit each other. The soldiers were falling all the while they were fighting back up the hill, and their horses got loose. Many of our people chased the horses, but I was not after horses; I was after Wasichus. When the soldiers got on top, there were not many of them left and they had no place to hide. They were fighting hard. We were told to crawl up on them, and we did. When we were close, someone yelled: "Let us go! This is a good day to die. Think of the helpless ones at home!" Then we all cried, "Hoka hey!" and rushed at them. I was

10

young then and quick on my feet, and I was one of the first to get in among the soldiers. They got up and fought very hard until not one of them was alive. They had a dog with them, and he started back up the road for the soldiers' town, howling as he ran. He was the only one left. I did not shoot at him because he looked too sweet,[5] but many did shoot, and he died full of arrows. So there was nobody left of the soldiers. Dead men and horses and wounded Indians were scattered all the way up the hill, and their blood was frozen, for a storm had come up and it was very cold and getting colder all the time. We left all the dead lying there, for the ground was solid, and we picked up our wounded and started back; but we lost most of them before we reached our camp at the mouth of the Peno. There was a big blizzard that night; and some of the wounded who did not die on the way, died after we got home. This was the time when Black Elk's father had his leg broken.

Black Elk Continues:

I am quite sure that I remember the time when my father came home with a broken leg that he got from killing so many Wasichus, and it seems that I can remember all about the battle too, but I think I could not. It must be the fear that I remember most. All this time I was not allowed to play very far away from our tepee, and my mother would say, "If you are not good the Wasichus will get you."

We must have broken camp at the mouth of the Peno soon after the battle, for I can remember my

[5] Because of its current colloquial usage as a vapid sentimentalism, the expression may well seem off key in the mouth of the grizzled old warrior.

father lying on a pony drag with bison robes all around him, like a baby, and my mother riding the pony. The snow was deep and it was very cold, and I remember sitting in another pony drag beside my father and mother, all wrapped up in fur. We were going away from where the soldiers were, and I do not know where we went, but it was west.

It was a hungry winter, for the deep snow made it hard to find the elk; and also many of the people went snowblind. We wandered a long time, and some of the bands got lost from each other. Then at last we were camping in the woods beside a creek somewhere, and the hunters came back with meat.

I think it was this same winter when a medicine man, by the name of Creeping, went around among the people curing snowblinds. He would put snow upon their eyes, and after he had sung a certain sacred song that he had heard in a dream, he would blow on the backs of their heads and they would see again, so I have heard. It was about the dragonfly that he sang, for that was where he got his power, they say.

When it was summer again we were camping on the Rosebud, and I did not feel so much afraid, because the Wasichus seemed farther away and there was peace there in the valley and there was plenty of meat. But all the boys from five or six years up were playing war. The little boys would gather together from the different bands of the tribe and fight each other with mud balls that they threw with willow sticks. And the big boys played the game called Throwing-Them-Off-Their-Horses, which is a battle all but the killing; and sometimes they got hurt. The horsebacks from the different bands would line up and charge upon each other, yelling; and when the

ponies came together on the run, they would rear and flounder and scream in a big dust, and the riders would seize each other, wrestling until one side had lost all its men, for those who fell upon the ground were counted dead.

When I was older, I, too, often played this game. We were always naked when we played it, just as warriors are when they go into battle if it is not too cold, because they are swifter without clothes. Once I fell off on my back right in the middle of a bed of prickly pears, and it took my mother a long while to pick all the stickers out of me. I was still too little to play war that summer, but I can remember watching the other boys, and I thought that when we all grew up and were big together, maybe we could kill all the Wasichus or drive them far away from our country.

It was in the Moon When the Cherries Turn Black (August) that all the people were talking again about a battle, and our warriors came back with many wounded. It was The Attacking of the Wagons,[6] and it made me afraid again, for we did not win that battle as we did the other one, and there was much mourning for the dead. Fire Thunder was in that fight too, and he can tell you how it was that day.

Fire Thunder Speaks:

It was very bad. There is a wide flat prairie with hills around it, and in the middle of this the Wasichus had put the boxes of their wagons in a circle, so that they could keep their mules there at night. There were not many Wasichus, but they were lying behind

[6] The Wagon Box Fight, which took place about six miles west of Fort Phil Kearney on August 2, 1867.

the boxes and they shot faster than they ever shot at
us before. We thought it was some new medicine of
great power that they had, for they shot so fast that
it was like tearing a blanket. Afterwards I learned
that it was because they had new guns that they
loaded from behind, and this was the first time they
used these guns.[7] We came on after sunrise. There
were many, many of us, and we meant to ride right
over them and rub them out. But our ponies were
afraid of the ring of fire the guns of the Wasichus
made, and would not go over. Our women were
watching us from the hills and we could hear them
singing and mourning whenever the shooting stopped.
We tried hard, but we could not do it, and there
were dead warriors and horses piled all around the
boxes and scattered over the plain. Then we left our
horses in a gulch and charged on foot, but it was
like green grass withering in a fire. So we picked up
our wounded and went away. I do not know how
many of our people were killed, but there were very
many. It was bad.

Black Elk Continues:

I do not remember where we camped that winter
but it must have been a time of peace and of plenty
to eat.

Standing Bear Speaks:

I am four years older than Black Elk, and he and
I have been good friends since boyhood. I know it
was on the Powder that we camped where there
were many cottonwood trees. Ponies like to eat the
bark of these trees and it is good for them. That

[7] Breech-loading Springfields.

was the winter when High Shirt's mother was killed by a big tree that fell on her tepee. It was a very windy night and there were noises that 'woke me, and then I heard that an old woman had been killed, and it was High Shirt's mother.

Black Elk Continues:

I was four years old then, and I think it must have been the next summer that I first heard the voices. It was a happy summer and nothing was afraid, because in the Moon When the Ponies Shed (May) word came from the Wasichus that there would be peace and that they would not use the road any more and that all the soldiers would go away. The soldiers did go away and their towns were torn down; and in the Moon of Falling Leaves (November), they made a treaty with Red Cloud that said our country would be ours as long as grass should grow and water flow. You can see that it is not the grass and the water that have forgotten.

Maybe it was not this summer when I first heard the voices, but I think it was, because I know it was before I played with bows and arrows or rode a horse, and I was out playing alone when I heard them. It was like somebody calling me, and I thought it was my mother, but there was nobody there. This happened more than once, and always made me afraid, so that I ran home.

It was when I was five years old that my Grandfather made me a bow and some arrows. The grass was young and I was horseback. A thunder storm was coming from where the sun goes down, and just as I was riding into the woods along a creek, there was a kingbird sitting on a limb. This was not a dream, it happened. And I was going to shoot at

15

the kingbird with the bow my Grandfather made, when the bird spoke and said: "The clouds all over are one-sided." Perhaps it meant that all the clouds were looking at me. And then it said: "Listen! A voice is calling you!" Then I looked up at the clouds, and two men were coming there, headfirst like arrows slanting down; and as they came, they sang a sacred song and the thunder was like drumming. I will sing it for you. The song and the drumming were like this:

"Behold, a sacred voice is calling you;
All over the sky a sacred voice is calling."

I sat there gazing at them, and they were coming from the place where the giant lives (north). But when they were very close to me, they wheeled about toward where the sun goes down, and suddenly they were geese. Then they were gone, and the rain came with a big wind and a roaring.

I did not tell this vision to any one. I liked to think about it, but I was afraid to tell it.

III

The Great Vision

What happened after that until the summer I was nine years old is not a story. There were winters and summers, and they were good; for the Wasichus had made their iron road[1] along the Platte and traveled there. This had cut the bison herd in two, but those that stayed in our country with us were more than could be counted, and we wandered without trouble in our land.

Now and then the voices would come back when I was out alone, like someone calling me, but what they wanted me to do I did not know. This did not happen very often, and when it did not happen, I forgot about it; for I was growing taller and was riding horses now and could shoot prairie chickens and rabbits with my bow. The boys of my people began very young to learn the ways of men, and no one taught us; we just learned by doing what we saw, and we were warriors at a time when boys now are like girls.

It was the summer when I was nine years old, and our people were moving slowly towards the Rocky

[1] The Union Pacific Railway.

Mountains. We camped one evening in a valley beside a little creek just before it ran into the Greasy Grass,[2] and there was a man by the name of Man Hip who liked me and asked me to eat with him in his tepee.

While I was eating, a voice came and said: "It is time; now they are calling you." The voice was so loud and clear that I believed it, and I thought I would just go where it wanted me to go. So I got right up and started. As I came out of the tepee, both my thighs began to hurt me, and suddenly it was like waking from a dream, and there wasn't any voice. So I went back into the tepee, but I didn't want to eat. Man Hip looked at me in a strange way and asked me what was wrong. I told him that my legs were hurting me.

The next morning the camp moved again, and I was riding with some boys. We stopped to get a drink from a creek, and when I got off my horse, my legs crumpled under me and I could not walk. So the boys helped me up and put me on my horse; and when we camped again that evening, I was sick. The next day the camp moved on to where the different bands of our people were coming together, and I rode in a pony drag, for I was very sick. Both my legs and both my arms were swollen badly and my face was all puffed up.

When we had camped again, I was lying in our tepee and my mother and father were sitting beside me. I could see out through the opening, and there two men were coming from the clouds, headfirst like arrows slanting down, and I knew they were the same that I had seen before. Each now carried a

[2] The Little Big Horn River.

long spear, and from the points of these a jagged lightning flashed. They came clear down to the ground this time and stood a little way off and looked at me and said: "Hurry! Come! Your Grandfathers are calling you!"

Then they turned and left the ground like arrows slanting upward from the bow. When I got up to follow, my legs did not hurt me any more and I was very light. I went outside the tepee, and yonder where the men with flaming spears were going, a little cloud was coming very fast. It came and stooped and took me and turned back to where it came from, flying fast. And when I looked down I could see my mother and my father yonder, and I felt sorry to be leaving them.

Then there was nothing but the air and the swiftness of the little cloud that bore me and those two men still leading up to where white clouds were piled like mountains on a wide blue plain, and in them thunder beings lived and leaped and flashed.

Now suddenly there was nothing but a world of cloud, and we three were there alone in the middle of a great white plain with snowy hills and mountains staring at us; and it was very still; but there were whispers.

Then the two men spoke together and they said: "Behold him, the being with four legs!"

I looked and saw a bay horse standing there, and he began to speak: "Behold me!" he said. "My life-history you shall see." Then he wheeled about to where the sun goes down, and said: "Behold them! Their history you shall know."

I looked, and there were twelve black horses yonder all abreast with necklaces of bison hoofs, and they were beautiful, but I was frightened, because

19

their manes were lightning and there was thunder in their nostrils.

Then the bay horse wheeled to where the great white giant lives (the north) and said: "Behold!" And yonder there were twelve white horses all abreast. Their manes were flowing like a blizzard wind and from their noses came a roaring, and all about them white geese soared and circled.

Then the bay wheeled round to where the sun shines continually (the east) and bade me look; and there twelve sorrel horses, with necklaces of elk's teeth, stood abreast with eyes that glimmered like the daybreak star and manes of morning light.

Then the bay wheeled once again to look upon the place where you are always facing (the south), and yonder stood twelve buckskins all abreast with horns upon their heads and manes that lived and grew like trees and grasses.

And when I had seen all these, the bay horse said: "Your Grandfathers are having a council. These shall take you; so have courage."

Then all the horses went into formation, four abreast—the blacks, the whites, the sorrels, and the buckskins—and stood behind the bay, who turned now to the west and neighed; and yonder suddenly the sky was terrible with a storm of plunging horses in all colors that shook the world with thunder, neighing back.

Now turning to the north the bay horse whinnied, and yonder all the sky roared with a mighty wind of running horses in all colors, neighing back.

And when he whinnied to the east, there too the sky was filled with glowing clouds of manes and tails of horses in all colors singing back. Then to the

20

south he called, and it was crowded with many colored, happy horses, nickering.

Then the bay horse spoke to me again and said: "See how your horses all come dancing!" I looked, and there were horses, horses everywhere—a whole skyful of horses dancing round me.

"Make haste!" the bay horse said; and we walked together side by side, while the blacks, the whites, the sorrels, and the buckskins followed, marching four by four.

I looked about me once again, and suddenly the dancing horses without number changed into animals of every kind and into all the fowls that are, and these fled back to the four quarters of the world from whence the horses came, and vanished.

Then as we walked, there was a heaped up cloud ahead that changed into a tepee, and a rainbow was the open door of it; and through the door I saw six old men sitting in a row.

The two men with the spears now stood beside me, one on either hand, and the horses took their places in their quarters, looking inward, four by four. And the oldest of the Grandfathers spoke with a kind voice and said: "Come right in and do not fear." And as he spoke, all the horses of the four quarters neighed to cheer me. So I went in and stood before the six, and they looked older than men can ever be—old like hills, like stars.

The oldest spoke again: "Your Grandfathers all over the world are having a council, and they have called you here to teach you." His voice was very kind, but I shook all over with fear now, for I knew that these were not old men, but the Powers of the World. And the first was the Power of the West; the second, of the North; the third, of the East; the

fourth, of the South; the fifth, of the Sky; the sixth, of the Earth. I knew this, and was afraid, until the first Grandfather spoke again: "Behold them yonder where the sun goes down, the thunder beings! You shall see, and have from them my power; and they shall take you to the high and lonely center of the earth that you may see; even to the place where the sun continually shines, they shall take you there to understand."

And as he spoke of understanding, I looked up and saw the rainbow leap with flames of many colors over me.

Now there was a wooden cup in his hand and it was full of water and in the water was the sky.

"Take this," he said. "It is the power to make live, and it is yours."

Now he had a bow in his hands. "Take this," he said. "It is the power to destroy, and it is yours."

Then he pointed to himself and said: "Look close at him who is your spirit now, for you are his body and his name is Eagle Wing Stretches."

And saying this, he got up very tall and started running toward where the sun goes down; and suddenly he was a black horse that stopped and turned and looked at me, and the horse was very poor and sick; his ribs stood out.

Then the second Grandfather, he of the North, arose with a herb of power in his hand, and said: "Take this and hurry." I took and held it toward the black horse yonder. He fattened and was happy and came prancing to his place again and was the first Grandfather sitting there.

The second Grandfather, he of the North, spoke again: "Take courage, younger brother," he said; "on earth a nation you shall make live, for yours

shall be the power of the white giant's wing, the
cleansing wing." Then he got up very tall and started
running toward the north; and when he turned to-
ward me, it was a white goose wheeling. I looked
about me now, and the horses in the west were
thunders and the horses of the north were geese.
And the second Grandfather sang two songs that
were like this:

"They are appearing, may you behold!
 They are appearing, may you behold!
 The thunder nation is appearing, behold!

 They are appearing, may you behold!
 They are appearing, may you behold!
 The white geese nation is appearing, behold!"

And now it was the third Grandfather who spoke,
he of where the sun shines continually. "Take cour-
age, younger brother," he said, "for across the earth
they shall take you!" Then he pointed to where the
daybreak star was shining, and beneath the star two
men were flying. "From them you shall have power,"
he said, "from them who have awakened all the
beings of the earth with roots and legs and wings."
And as he said this, he held in his hand a peace pipe
which had a spotted eagle outstretched upon the
stem; and this eagle seemed alive, for it was poised
there, fluttering, and its eyes were looking at me.
"With this pipe," the Grandfather said, "you shall
walk upon the earth, and whatever sickens there
you shall make well." Then he pointed to a man
who was bright red all over, the color of good and
of plenty, and as he pointed, the red man lay down
and rolled and changed into a bison that got up and

23

galloped toward the sorrel horses of the east, and they too turned to bison, fat and many.

And now the fourth Grandfather spoke, he of the place where you are always facing (the south), whence comes the power to grow. "Younger brother," he said, "with the powers of the four quarters you shall walk, a relative. Behold, the living center of a nation I shall give you, and with it many you shall save." And I saw that he was holding in his hand a bright red stick that was alive, and as I looked it sprouted at the top and sent forth branches, and on the branches many leaves came out and murmured and in the leaves the birds began to sing. And then for just a little while I thought I saw beneath it in the shade the circled villages of people and every living thing with roots or legs or wings, and all were happy. "It shall stand in the center of the nation's circle," said the Grandfather, "a cane to walk with and a people's heart; and by your powers you shall make it blossom."

Then when he had been still a little while to hear the birds sing, he spoke again: "Behold the earth!" So I looked down and saw it lying yonder like a hoop of peoples, and in the center bloomed the holy stick that was a tree, and where it stood there crossed two roads, a red one and a black. "From where the giant lives (the north) to where you always face (the south) the red road goes, the road of good," the Grandfather said, "and on it shall your nation walk. The black road goes from where the thunder beings live (the west) to where the sun continually shines (the east), a fearful road, a road of troubles and of war. On this also you shall walk, and from it you shall have the power to destroy a people's foes. In four ascents you shall walk the earth with power."

I think he meant that I should see four generations, counting me, and now I am seeing the third.

Then he rose very tall and started running toward the south, and was an elk; and as he stood among the buckskins yonder, they too were elks.

Now the fifth Grandfather spoke, the oldest of them all, the Spirit of the Sky. "My boy," he said, "I have sent for you and you have come. My power you shall see!" He stretched his arms and turned into a spotted eagle hovering. "Behold," he said, "all the wings of the air shall come to you, and they and the winds and the stars shall be like relatives. You shall go across the earth with my power." Then the eagle soared above my head and fluttered there; and suddenly the sky was full of friendly wings all coming toward me.

Now I knew the sixth Grandfather was about to speak, he who was the Spirit of the Earth, and I saw that he was very old, but more as men are old. His hair was long and white, his face was all in wrinkles and his eyes were deep and dim. I stared at him, for it seemed I knew him somehow; and as I stared, he slowly changed, for he was growing backwards into youth, and when he had become a boy, I knew that he was myself with all the years that would be mine at last. When he was old again, he said: "My boy, have courage, for my power shall be yours, and you shall need it, for your nation on the earth will have great troubles. Come."

He rose and tottered out through the rainbow door, and as I followed I was riding on the bay horse who had talked to me at first and led me to that place.

Then the bay horse stopped and faced the black

horses of the west, and a voice said: "They have given you the cup of water to make live the greening day, and also the bow and arrow to destroy." The bay neighed, and the twelve black horses came and stood behind me, four abreast.

The bay faced the sorrels of the east, and I saw that they had morning stars upon their foreheads and they were very bright. And the voice said: "They have given you the sacred pipe and the power that is peace, and the good red day." The bay neighed, and the twelve sorrels stood behind me, four abreast.

My horse now faced the buckskins of the south, and a voice said: "They have given you the sacred stick and your nation's hoop, and the yellow day; and in the center of the hoop you shall set the stick and make it grow into a shielding tree, and bloom." The bay neighed, and the twelve buckskins came and stood behind me, four abreast.

Then I knew that there were riders on all the horses there behind me, and a voice said: "Now you shall walk the black road with these; and as you walk, all the nations that have roots or legs or wings shall fear you."

So I started, riding toward the east down the fearful road, and behind me came the horsebacks four abreast—the blacks, the whites, the sorrels, and the buckskins—and far away above the fearful road the daybreak star was rising very dim.

I looked below me where the earth was silent in a sick green light, and saw the hills look up afraid and the grasses on the hills and all the animals; and everywhere about me were the cries of frightened birds and sounds of fleeing wings. I was the chief of all the heavens riding there, and when I looked behind me, all the twelve black horses reared and

plunged and thundered and their manes and tails were whirling hail and their nostrils snorted lightning. And when I looked below again, I saw the slant hail falling and the long, sharp rain, and where we passed, the trees bowed low and all the hills were dim.

Now the earth was bright again as we rode. I could see the hills and valleys and the creeks and rivers passing under. We came above a place where three streams made a big one—a source of mighty waters[3]—and something terrible was there. Flames were rising from the waters and in the flames a blue man lived. The dust was floating all about him in the air, the grass was short and withered, the trees were wilting, two-legged and four-legged beings lay there thin and panting, and wings too weak to fly.

Then the black horse riders shouted "Hoka hey!" and charged down upon the blue man, but were driven back. And the white troop shouted, charging, and was beaten; then the red troop and the yellow.

And when each had failed, they all cried together: "Eagle Wing Stretches, hurry!" And all the world was filled with voices of all kinds that cheered me, so I charged. I had the cup of water in one hand and in the other was the bow that turned into a spear as the bay and I swooped down, and the spear's head was sharp lightning. It stabbed the blue man's heart, and as it struck I could hear the thunder rolling and many voices that cried "Un-hee!," meaning I had killed. The flames died. The trees and grasses were not withered any more and murmured happily together, and every living being cried in gladness with

[3] Black Elk thinks this was the Three Forks of the Missouri.

27

whatever voice it had. Then the four troops of horsemen charged down and struck the dead body of the blue man, counting coup; and suddenly it was only a harmless turtle.

You see, I had been riding with the storm clouds, and had come to earth as rain, and it was drouth that I had killed with the power that the Six Grandfathers gave me. So we were riding on the earth now down along the river flowing full from the source of waters, and soon I saw ahead the circled village of a people in the valley. And a Voice said: "Behold a nation; it is yours. Make haste, Eagle Wing Stretches!"

I entered the village, riding, with the four horse troops behind me—the blacks, the whites, the sorrels, and the buckskins; and the place was filled with moaning and with mourning for the dead. The wind was blowing from the south like fever, and when I looked around I saw that in nearly every tepee the women and the children and the men lay dying with the dead.

So I rode around the circle of the village, looking in upon the sick and dead, and I felt like crying as I rode. But when I looked behind me, all the women and the children and the men were getting up and coming forth with happy faces.

And a Voice said: "Behold, they have given you the center of the nation's hoop to make it live."

So I rode to the center of the village, with the horse troops in their quarters round about me, and there the people gathered. And the Voice said: "Give them now the flowering stick that they may flourish, and the sacred pipe that they may know the power that is peace, and the wing of the white giant that

28

they may have endurance and face all winds with courage."

So I took the bright red stick and at the center of the nation's hoop I thrust it in the earth. As it touched the earth it leaped mightily in my hand and was a waga chun, the rustling tree,[4] very tall and full of leafy branches and of all birds singing. And beneath it all the animals were mingling with the people like relatives and making happy cries. The women raised their tremolo of joy, and the men shouted all together: "Here we shall raise our children and be as little chickens under the mother sheo's[5] wing."

Then I heard the white wind blowing gently through the tree and singing there, and from the east the sacred pipe came flying on its eagle wings, and stopped before me there beneath the tree, spreading deep peace around it.

Then the daybreak star was rising, and a Voice said: "It shall be a relative to them; and who shall see it, shall see much more, for thence comes wisdom; and those who do not see it shall be dark." And all the people raised their faces to the east, and the star's light fell upon them, and all the dogs barked loudly and the horses whinnied.

Then when the many little voices ceased, the great Voice said: "Behold the circle of the nation's hoop, for it is holy, being endless, and thus all powers shall be one power in the people without end. Now they shall break camp and go forth upon the red road, and your Grandfathers shall walk with them." So the people broke camp and took the good road with

[4] The cottonwood.
[5] Prairie hen.

the white wing on their faces, and the order of their going was like this:

First, the black horse riders with the cup of water; and the white horse riders with the white wing and the sacred herb; and the sorrel riders with the holy pipe; and the buckskins with the flowering stick. And after these the little children and the youths and maidens followed in a band.

Second, came the tribe's four chieftains, and their band was all young men and women.

Third, the nation's four advisers leading men and women neither young nor old.

Fourth, the old men hobbling with their canes and looking to the earth.

Fifth, old women hobbling with their canes and looking to the earth.

Sixth, myself all alone upon the bay with the bow and arrows that the First Grandfather gave me. But I was not the last; for when I looked behind me there were ghosts of people like a trailing fog as far as I could see—grandfathers of grandfathers and grandmothers of grandmothers without number. And over these a great Voice—the Voice that was the South—lived, and I could feel it silent.

And as we went the Voice behind me said: "Behold a good nation walking in a sacred manner in a good land!"

Then I looked up and saw that there were four ascents ahead, and these were generations I should know. Now we were on the first ascent, and all the land was green. And as the long line climbed, all the old men and women raised their hands, palms forward, to the far sky yonder and began to croon a song together, and the sky ahead was filled with clouds of baby faces.

When we came to the end of the first ascent we camped in the sacred circle as before, and in the center stood the holy tree, and still the land about us was all green.

Then we started on the second ascent, marching as before, and still the land was green, but it was getting steeper. And as I looked ahead, the people changed into elks and bison and all four-footed beings and even into fowls, all walking in a sacred manner on the good red road together. And I myself was a spotted eagle soaring over them. But just before we stopped to camp at the end of that ascent, all the marching animals grew restless and afraid that they were not what they had been, and began sending forth voices of trouble, calling to their chiefs. And when they camped at the end of that ascent, I looked down and saw that leaves were falling from the holy tree.

And the Voice said: "Behold your nation, and remember what your Six Grandfathers gave you, for thenceforth your people walk in difficulties."

Then the people broke camp again, and saw the black road before them towards where the sun goes down, and black clouds coming yonder; and they did not want to go but could not stay. And as they walked the third ascent, all the animals and fowls that were the people ran here and there, for each one seemed to have his own little vision that he followed and his own rules; and all over the universe I could hear the winds at war like wild beasts fighting.[6]

[6] At this point Black Elk remarked: "I think we are near that place now, and I am afraid something very bad is going to happen all over the world." He cannot read and knows nothing of world affairs.

And when we reached the summit of the third ascent and camped, the nation's hoop was broken like a ring of smoke that spreads and scatters and the holy tree seemed dying and all its birds were gone. And when I looked ahead I saw that the fourth ascent would be terrible.

Then when the people were getting ready to begin the fourth ascent, the Voice spoke like some one weeping, and it said: "Look there upon your nation." And when I looked down, the people were all changed back to human, and they were thin, their faces sharp, for they were starving. Their ponies were only hide and bones, and the holy tree was gone.

And as I looked and wept, I saw that there stood on the north side of the starving camp a sacred man who was painted red all over his body, and he held a spear as he walked into the center of the people, and there he lay down and rolled. And when he got up, it was a fat bison standing there, and where the bison stood a sacred herb sprang up right where the tree had been in the center of the nation's hoop. The herb grew and bore four blossoms on a single stem while I was looking—a blue,[7] a white, a scarlet, and a yellow—and the bright rays of these flashed to the heavens.

I know now what this meant, that the bison were the gift of a good spirit and were our strength, but we should lose them, and from the same good spirit we must find another strength. For the people all seemed better when the herb had grown and bloomed, and the horses raised their tails and neighed and pranced around, and I could see a light breeze

[7] Blue as well as black may be used to represent the power of the west.

going from the north among the people like a ghost; and suddenly the flowering tree was there again at the center of the nation's hoop where the four-rayed herb had blossomed.

I was still the spotted eagle floating, and I could see that I was already in the fourth ascent and the people were camping yonder at the top of the third long rise. It was dark and terrible about me, for all the winds of the world were fighting. It was like rapid gun-fire and like whirling smoke, and like women and children wailing and like horses screaming all over the world.

I could see my people yonder running about, setting the smoke-flap poles and fastening down their tepees against the wind, for the storm cloud was coming on them very fast and black, and there were frightened swallows without number fleeing before the cloud.

Then a song of power came to me and I sang it there in the midst of that terrible place where I was. It went like this:

A good nation I will make live.
This the nation above has said.
They have given me the power to make over.

And when I had sung this, a Voice said: "To the four quarters you shall run for help, and nothing shall be strong before you. Behold him!"

Now I was on my bay horse again, because the horse is of the earth, and it was there my power would be used. And as I obeyed the Voice and looked, there was a horse all skin and bones yonder in the west, a faded brownish black. And a Voice there said: "Take this and make him over; and it

33

was the four-rayed herb that I was holding in my hand. So I rode above the poor horse in a circle, and as I did this I could hear the people yonder calling for spirit power, "A-hey! a-hey! a-hey! a-hey!" Then the poor horse neighed and rolled and got up, and he was a big, shiny, black stallion with dapples all over him and his mane about him like a cloud. He was the chief of all the horses; and when he snorted, it was a flash of lightning and his eyes were like the sunset star. He dashed to the west and neighed, and the west was filled with a dust of hoofs, and horses without number, shiny black, came plunging from the dust. Then he dashed toward the north and neighed, and to the east and to the south, and the dust clouds answered, giving forth their plunging horses without number—whites and sorrels and buckskins, fat, shiny, rejoicing in their fleetness and their strength. It was beautiful, but it was also terrible.

Then they all stopped short, rearing, and were standing in a great hoop about their black chief at the center, and were still. And as they stood, four virgins, more beautiful than women of the earth can be, came through the circle, dressed in scarlet, one from each of the four quarters, and stood about the great black stallion in their places; and one held the wooden cup of water, and one the white wing, and one the pipe, and one the nation's hoop. All the universe was silent, listening; and then the great black stallion raised his voice and sang. The song he sang was this:

"My horses, prancing they are coming.
My horses, neighing they are coming;
Prancing, they are coming.

34

All over the universe they come.
They will dance; may you behold them.
 (4 times)
A horse nation, they will dance. May you be-
 hold them." (4 times)

His voice was not loud, but it went all over the
universe and filled it. There was nothing that did
not hear, and it was more beautiful than anything
can be. It was so beautiful that nothing anywhere
could keep from dancing. The virgins danced, and
all the circled horses. The leaves on the trees, the
grasses on the hills and in the valleys, the waters
in the creeks and in the rivers and the lakes, the
four-legged and the two-legged and the wings of the
air—all danced together to the music of the stal-
lion's song.

And when I looked down upon my people yon-
der, the cloud passed over, blessing them with
friendly rain, and stood in the east with a flaming
rainbow over it.

Then all the horses went singing back to their
places beyond the summit of the fourth ascent, and
all things sang along with them as they walked.

And a Voice said: "All over the universe they
have finished a day of happiness." And looking
down, I saw that the whole wide circle of the day
was beautiful and green, with all fruits growing and
all things kind and happy.

Then a Voice said: "Behold this day, for it is
yours to make. Now you shall stand upon the center
of the earth to see, for there they are taking you."

I was still on my bay horse, and once more I felt
the riders of the west, the north, the east, the south,
behind me in formation, as before, and we were

going east. I looked ahead and saw the mountains there with rocks and forests on them, and from the mountains flashed all colors upward to the heavens. Then I was standing on the highest mountain of them all, and round about beneath me was the whole hoop of the world.[8] And while I stood there I saw more than I can tell and I understood more than I saw; for I was seeing in a sacred manner the shapes of all things in the spirit, and the shape of all shapes as they must live together like one being. And I saw that the sacred hoop of my people was one of many hoops that made one circle, wide as daylight and as starlight, and in the center grew one mighty flowering tree to shelter all the children of one mother and one father. And I saw that it was holy.

Then as I stood there, two men were coming from the east, head first like arrows flying, and between them rose the daybreak star. They came and gave a herb to me and said: "With this on earth you shall undertake anything and do it." It was the day-break-star herb, the herb of understanding, and they told me to drop it on the earth. I saw it falling far, and when it struck the earth it rooted and grew and flowered, four blossoms on one stem, a blue, a white, a scarlet, and a yellow; and the rays from these streamed upward to the heavens so that all creatures saw it and in no place was there darkness.

Then the Voice said: "Your Six Grandfathers—now you shall go back to them."

I had not noticed how I was dressed until now, and I saw that I was painted red all over, and my

[8] Black Elk said the mountain he stood upon in his vision was Harney Peak in the Black Hills. "But anywhere is the center of the world," he added.

joints were painted black, with white stripes be-
tween the joints. My bay had lightning stripes all
over him, and his mane was cloud. And when I
breathed, my breath was lightning.

Now two men were leading me, head first like
arrows slanting upward—the two that brought me
from the earth. And as I followed on the bay, they
turned into four flocks of geese that flew in circles,
one above each quarter, sending forth a sacred voice
as they flew: Br-r-r-p, br-r-r-p, br-r-r-p, br-r-r-p!

Then I saw ahead the rainbow flaming above the
tepee of the Six Grandfathers, built and roofed with
cloud and sewed with thongs of lightning; and
underneath it were all the wings of the air and under
them the animals and men. All these were rejoicing,
and thunder was like happy laughter.

As I rode in through the rainbow door, there were
cheering voices from all over the universe, and I
saw the Six Grandfathers sitting in a row, with their
arms held toward me and their hands, palms out;
and behind them in the cloud were faces thronging,
without number, of the people yet to be.

"He has triumphed!" cried the six together,
making thunder. And as I passed before them there,
each gave again the gift that he had given me be-
fore—the cup of water and the bow and arrows,
the power to make live and to destroy; the white
wing of cleansing and the healing herb; the sacred
pipe; the flowering stick. And each one spoke in turn
from west to south, explaining what he gave as he
had done before, and as each one spoke he melted
down into the earth and rose again; and as each
did this, I felt nearer to the earth.

Then the oldest of them all said: "Grandson,
all over the universe you have seen. Now you

shall go back with power to the place from whence you came, and it shall happen yonder that hundreds shall be sacred, hundreds shall be flames! Behold!"

I looked below and saw my people there, and all were well and happy except one, and he was lying like the dead—and that one was myself. Then the oldest Grandfather sang, and his song was like this:

"There is someone lying on earth in a sacred manner.
There is someone—on earth he lies.
In a sacred manner I have made him to walk."

Now the tepee, built and roofed with cloud, began to sway back and forth as in a wind, and the flaming rainbow door was growing dimmer. I could hear voices of all kinds crying from outside: "Eagle Wing Stretches is coming forth! Behold him!"

When I went through the door, the face of the day of earth was appearing with the daybreak star upon its forehead; and the sun leaped up and looked upon me, and I was going forth alone.

And as I walked alone, I heard the sun singing as it arose, and it sang like this:

"With visible face I am appearing.
In a sacred manner I appear.
For the greening earth a pleasantness I make.
The center of the nation's hoop I have made pleasant.
With visible face, behold me!
The four-leggeds and two-leggeds, I have made them to walk;

The wings of the air, I have made them to fly.
With visible face I appear.
My day, I have made it holy."

When the singing stopped, I was feeling lost and very lonely. Then a Voice above me said: "Look back!" It was a spotted eagle that was hovering over me and spoke. I looked, and where the flaming rainbow tepee, built and roofed with cloud, had been, I saw only the tall rock mountain at the center of the world.

I was all alone on a broad plain now with my feet upon the earth, alone but for the spotted eagle guarding me. I could see my people's village far ahead, and I walked very fast, for I was homesick now. Then I saw my own tepee, and inside I saw my mother and my father, bending over a sick boy that was myself. And as I entered the tepee, some one was saying: "The boy is coming to; you had better give him some water."

Then I was sitting up; and I was sad because my mother and my father didn't seem to know I had been so far away.

IV

The Bison Hunt

When I got back to my father and mother and was sitting up there in our tepee, my face was still all puffed and my legs and arms were badly swollen; but I felt good all over and wanted to get right up and run around. My parents would not let me. They told me I had been sick twelve days, lying like dead all the while, and that Whirlwind Chaser, who was Standing Bear's uncle and a medicine man, had brought me back to life. I knew it was the Grandfathers in the Flaming Rainbow Tepee who had cured me; but I felt afraid to say so. My father gave Whirlwind Chaser the best horse he had for making me well, and many people came to look at me, and there was much talk about the great power of Whirlwind Chaser who had made me well all at once when I was almost the same as dead.

Everybody was glad that I was living; but as I lay there thinking about the wonderful place where I had been and all that I had seen, I was very sad; for it seemed to me that everybody ought to know about it, but I was afraid to tell, because I knew that nobody would believe me, little as I was, for I was only nine years old. Also, as I lay there think-

ing of my vision, I could see it all again and feel the meaning with a part of me like a strange power glowing in my body; but when the part of me that talks would try to make words for the meaning, it would be like fog and get away from me.

I am sure now that I was then too young to understand it all, and that I only felt it. It was the pictures I remembered and the words that went with them; for nothing I have ever seen with my eyes was so clear and bright as what my vision showed me; and no words that I have ever heard with my ears were like the words I heard. I did not have to remember these things; they have remembered themselves all these years. It was as I grew older that the meanings came clearer and clearer out of the pictures and the words; and even now I know that more was shown to me than I can tell.

That evening of the day when I came back, Whirlwind Chaser, who had got a great name and a good horse for curing me, came over to our tepee. He sat down and looked at me a long time in a strange way, and then he said to my father: "Your boy there is sitting in a sacred manner. I do not know what it is, but there is something special for him to do, for just as I came in I could see a power like a light all through his body."

While he was looking hard at me, I wanted to get up and run away, for I was afraid he might look right into me and see my vision there and tell it wrong, and then maybe all the people would think that I was crazy. For a long while after that, whenever I saw Whirlwind Chaser coming, I would run away and hide for fear he might see into me and tell.

The next morning all the swelling had left my face

and legs and arms, and I felt well as ever; but everything around me seemed strange and as though it were far away. I remember that for twelve days after that I wanted to be alone, and it seemed I did not belong to my people. They were almost like strangers. I would be out alone away from the village and the other boys, and I would look around to the four quarters, thinking of my vision and wishing I could get back there again. I would go home to eat, but I could not make myself eat much; and my father and mother thought that I was sick yet; but I was not. I was only homesick for the place where I had been.

I could not tell what I had seen and heard even to my mother's father, Refuse-To-Go, although before that I used to think that I could tell him anything, for he liked everything a boy could like, and there was no end to the wonderful things he would tell. It was he who made the first bow I ever had, and he always had more arrows ready for me when I had lost all those that he had given me. I loved my father, but Refuse-To-Go was different, and I used to be with him a great deal. This was the first thing I could not tell him.

One day during this time I was out with the bow and arrows my Grandfather had made for me, and as I walked along thinking of my vision, suddenly I felt queer, and for a little while it seemed that the bow and arrows were those that the First Grandfather in the Flaming Rainbow Tepee had given me. Then they were only those that Refuse-To-Go had made, and I felt foolish and tried to make myself think it was all only a dream anyway. So I thought I would forget about it and shoot something. There was a bush and a little bird sitting in it; but just as

42

I was going to shoot, I felt queer again, and remembered that I was to be like a relative with the birds. So I did not shoot. Then I went on down toward a creek, feeling foolish because I had let the little bird go, and when I saw a green frog sitting there, I just shot him right away. But when I picked him up by the legs, I thought: "Now I have killed him," and it made me want to cry.

Standing Bear Speaks:

I remember the time when my friend here was sick. I was four years older than he was. I am a Minneconjou, but our mothers were cousins and we used to play together when our bands were camping in one place. It was at the headwaters of the Greasy Grass (Little Big Horn). Everybody in the village was well, and so was Black Elk. The next thing I heard was that he was dying and just breathing a little. Everybody was excited over it, and they sent for medicine to other bands, but nobody knew what the sickness was. I saw him during this time. He looked dead, and everybody was talking about him. Then he was well all at once, and everybody wondered and talked about it.

I remember too how it was after he got up. Right after that we moved camp to the mouth of Willow Creek, south about two days, and while the village was moving, I rode back to where the smaller boys were in the rear, for I wanted to see my young friend. I said to him: "How, younger brother! You got well after all!" And he said: "How! Yes, I am not sick at all now!" But as we rode along together and talked, he was not like a boy. He was more like an old man. And I can remember his father talking to my father in our tepee while we were eat-

ing one evening. He said something like this: "Since my boy was sick, he is not the same boy. He has queer ways and he does not like to be at home. I feel sorry about the way he is, poor boy!"

Then we went on a big hunt and the people did not talk about it any more.

Black Elk Continues:

Yes, we went on a big hunt after we had been at Willow Creek awhile, and it helped me to quit thinking about my vision all the time.

One morning the crier came around the circle of the village calling out that we were going to break camp. The advisers were in the council tepee, and he cried to them: "The advisers, come forth to the center and bring your fires along." It was their duty to save fire for the people, because we had no matches then.

"Now take it down, down!" the crier shouted. And all the people began taking down their tepees, and packing them on pony drags.

Then the crier said: "Many bison, I have heard; many bison, I have heard! Your children, you must take care of them!" He meant to keep the children close while traveling, so that they would not scare the bison.

Then we broke camp and started in formation, the four advisers first, a crier behind them, the chiefs next, and then the people with the loaded pony drags in a long line, and the herd of ponies following. I was riding near the rear with some of the smaller boys, and when the people were going up a long hill, I looked ahead and it made me feel queer again for a little while, because I remembered the nation

walking in a sacred manner on the red road in my vision. But this was different, and I forgot about it soon, for something exciting was going to happen, and even the ponies seemed to know.

After we had been traveling awhile, we came to a place where there were many turnips growing, and the crier said: "Take off your loads and let your horses rest. Take your sticks and dig turnips for yourselves." And while the people were doing this, the advisers sat on a hill nearby and smoked. Then the crier shouted: "Put on your loads!" and soon the village was moving again.

When the sun was high, the advisers found a place to camp where there was wood and also water; and while the women were cooking all around the circle I heard people saying that the scouts were returning, and over the top of a hill I saw three horsebacks coming. They rode to the council tepee in the middle of the village and all the people were going there to hear. I went there too and got up close so that I could look in between the legs of the men. The crier came out of the council tepee and said, speaking to the people for the scouts: "I have protected you; in return you shall give me many gifts." The scouts then sat down before the door of the tepee and one of the advisers filled the sacred pipe with chacun sha sha, the bark of the red willow, and set it on a bison chip in front of him, because the bison was sacred and gave us both food and shelter. Then he lit the pipe, offered it to the four quarters, to the Spirit above and to Mother Earth, and passing it to the scouts he said: "The nation has depended upon you. Whatever you have seen, maybe it is for the good of the people you have seen." The scouts smoked, meaning that they would tell the truth. Then

45

the adviser said: "At what place have you stood and seen the good? Report it to me and I will be glad."

One of the scouts answered: "You know where we started from. We went and reached the top of a hill and there we saw a small herd of bison." He pointed as he spoke.

The adviser said: "Maybe on the other side of that you have seen the good. Report it." The scout answered: "On the other side of that we saw a second and larger herd of bison."

Then the adviser said: "I shall be thankful to you. Tell me all that you have seen out there."

The scout replied: "On the other side of that there was nothing but bison all over the country."

And the adviser said: "Hetchetu aloh!"[1]

Then the crier shouted like singing: "Your knives shall be sharpened, your arrows shall be sharpened. Make ready, make haste; your horses make ready! We shall go forth with arrows. Plenty of meat we shall make!"

Everybody began sharpening knives and arrows and getting the best horses ready for the great making of meat.

Then we started for where the bison were. The soldier band went first, riding twenty abreast, and anybody who dared go ahead of them would get knocked off his horse. They kept order, and everybody had to obey. After them came the hunters, riding five abreast. The people came up in the rear. Then the head man of the advisers went around picking out the best hunters with the fastest horses, and to these he said: "Good young warriors, my

[1] "It is so indeed."

relatives, your work I know is good. What you do is good always; so to-day you shall feed the helpless. Perhaps there are some old and feeble people without sons, or some who have little children and no man. You shall help these, and whatever you kill shall be theirs." This was a great honor for young men.

Then when we had come near to where the bison were, the hunters circled around them, and the cry went up, as in a battle, "Hoka hey!" which meant to charge. Then there was a great dust and everybody shouted and all the hunters went in to kill— every man for himself. They were all nearly naked, with their quivers full of arrows hanging on their left sides, and they would ride right up to a bison and shoot him behind the left shoulder. Some of the arrows would go in up to the feathers and sometimes those that struck no bones went right straight through. Everybody was very happy.

Standing Bear Speaks:

I remember that hunt, for before that time I had only killed a calf. I was thirteen years old and supposed to be a man, so I made up my mind I'd get a yearling. One of them went down a draw and I raced after him on my pony. My first shot did not seem to hurt him at all; but my pony kept right after him, and the second arrow went in half way. I think I hit his heart, for he began to wobble as he ran and blood came out of his nose. Hunters cried "Yuhoo!" once when they killed, but this was my first big bison, and I just kept on yelling "Yuhoo!" People must have thought I was killing a whole herd, the way I yelled. When he went down,

47

I got off my horse and began butchering him myself, and I was very happy. All over the flat, as far as I could see, there were men butchering bison now, and the women and the old men who could not hunt were coming up to help. And all the women were making the tremolo of joy for what the warriors had given them. That was in the Moon of Red Cherries (July). It was a great killing.

Black Elk Continues:

I was well enough to go along on my pony, but I was not old enough to hunt. So we little boys scouted around and watched the hunters; and when we would see a bunch of bison coming, we would yell "Yuhoo" like the others, but nobody noticed us.

When the butchering was all over, they hung the meat across the horses' backs and fastened it with strips of fresh bison hide. On the way back to the village all the hunting horses were loaded, and we little boys who could not wait for the feast helped ourselves to all the raw liver we wanted. Nobody got cross when we did this.

During this time, women back at camp were cutting long poles and forked sticks to make drying racks for the meat. When the hunters got home they threw their meat in piles on the leaves of trees.

Then the advisers all went back into the council tepee, and from all directions the people came bringing gifts of meat to them, and the advisers all cried "Hya-a-a-a!," after which they sang for those who had brought them the good gifts. And when they had eaten all they could, the crier shouted to the people: "All come home! It is more than I can eat!"

And people from all over the camp came to get a little of the meat that was left over.

The women were all busy cutting the meat into strips and hanging it on the racks to dry. You could see red meat hanging everywhere. The people feasted all night long and danced and sang. Those were happy times.

There was a war game that we little boys played after a big hunt. We went out a little way from the village and built some grass tepees, playing we were enemies and this was our village. We had an adviser, and when it got dark he would order us to go and steal some dried meat from the big people. He would hold a stick up to us and we had to bite off a piece of it. If we bit a big piece we had to get a big piece of meat, and if we bit a little piece, we did not have to get so much. Then we started for the big people's village, crawling on our bellies, and when we got back without getting caught, we would have a big feast and a dance and make kill talks, telling of our brave deeds like warriors. Once, I remember, I had no brave deed to tell. I crawled up to a leaning tree beside a tepee and there was meat hanging on the limbs. I wanted a tongue I saw up there in the moonlight, so I climbed up. But just as I was about to reach it, the man in the tepee yelled "Ye-a-a!" He was saying this to his dog, who was stealing some meat too, but I thought the man had seen me, and I was so scared I fell out of the tree and ran away crying.

Then we used to have what we called a chapped breast dance. Our adviser would look us over to see whose breast was burned most from not having it covered with the robe we wore; and the boy chosen would lead the dance while we all sang like this:

"I have a chapped breast.
My breast is red.
My breast is yellow."

And we practiced endurance too. Our adviser would
put dry sunflower seeds on our wrists. These were lit
at the top, and we had to let them burn clear down
to the skin. They hurt and made sores, but if we
knocked them off or cried Owh!, we would be called
women.

V

At the Soldiers' Town

After all the meat was dried, the six bands[1] of our
nation that had come together about the time when
the great vision came to me, broke camp at the
mouth of Willow Creek and scattered in all direc-
tions. A small part of our band, the Ogalalas, started
south for the Soldiers' Town[2] on Smoky Earth River
(the White), for some of our relatives were there
and we wanted to see them and have a feast of
aguiapi and paezhuta sapa with chahumpi ska in it.[3]
All the rest of the Ogalalas stayed in that country
with Crazy Horse, who would have nothing to do
with the Wasichus. This was late in the Moon When
the Cherries are Ripe (July) and we boys had a
good time playing. There were not many boys in our
small band, and we all played together. I had quit
thinking about my vision. The queer feeling had left
me and I was not bashful any more; but whenever

[1] Ogalalas, Brules, Sans Arcs, Black Kettles, Hunkpapas,
Minneconjous.

[2] Fort Robinson.

[3] Aguiapi, "brown all over," bread. Paezhuta sapa, "black
medicine," coffee. Chahumpi ska, "white juice of the tree,"
sugar.

51

a thunder storm was coming I felt happy, as though somebody were coming to visit me.

We camped first on Powder River, then on the headwaters of the north fork of Good River (the Cheyenne) where there is a big butte that we called Sits-With-Young-One, because it has a little butte beside it. Then we camped on Driftwood Creek, then on the Plain of Pine Trees, and next on Plum Creek. When we got there, the plums were turning red, but they were not quite ripe yet. My grandfather went out and got some big red ones and they tasted good. When we got to War Bonnet Creek, which is not very far from the Soldiers' Town, my aunt and other relatives were there waiting for us with bread and coffee, and we had a big feast. I was sick all that night, and the next day my parents made me ride on a pony drag, because they were afraid I would surely die this time. But I think it was only too much bread and coffee, and maybe the plums. We camped again at Hips Hill, and by this time most of our people from the Soldiers' Town were among us. The next day about twenty tepees of us went on, and the rest stayed back. We camped with our relatives by White Butte near the Soldiers' Town and stayed there all winter, and we had a good time sliding down hill with sleds made out of bison jaws and ribs tied together with rawhide.

I was ten years old that winter, and that was the first time I ever saw a Wasichu. At first I thought they all looked sick, and I was afraid they might just begin to fight us any time, but I got used to them.

That winter one of our boys climbed the flagpole and chopped it off near the top. This almost made bad trouble, for the soldiers surrounded us with their

guns; but Red Cloud, who was living there, stood right in the middle without a weapon and made speeches to the Wasichus and to us. He said the boy who did it must be punished, and he told the Wasichus it was foolish for men to want to shoot grown people because their little boys did foolish things in play; and he asked them if they ever did foolish things for fun when they were boys. So nothing happened after all.

Red Cloud was a great chief, and he was an Ogalala. But at this time he was through with fighting. After the treaty he made with the Wasichus five years before (1868) he never fought again, and he was living with his band, the Bad Faces, at the Soldier's Town. Crazy Horse was an Ogalala too, and I think he was the greatest chief of all.

In the Moon of the Red Grass Appearing (April) about thirty tepees of us broke camp and started for the Black Hills to cut tepee poles. We followed down Horse-Head-Cutting Creek to its mouth, and while we were camped there one day I was away from the village alone, when I heard a spotted eagle whistle. I looked up and there he was, hovering over me. The queer feeling came back very strong, and for a little while it seemed that I was in the world of my vision again.

From there we moved on to Buffalo Gap at the foot of the Hills, and my father and I went out alone to look for deer. We climbed up through the timber to the top of a big hill, and it was hard for my father, who was lame from the wound he got in the Battle of the Hundred Slain. When we were on top, my father looked down and said: "There are some yonder. You stay here, and I will go around them." Then the queer feeling came back, and I said with-

out knowing why I said it: "No, father, stay here; for they are bringing them to us." He looked at me hard, and said: "Who is bringing them?" I could not answer; and after he had looked hard at me again, he said: "All right, son." So we lay down there in the grass and waited. They did come to us, and my father got two of them.

While we were butchering and I was eating some liver, I felt sorry that we had killed these animals and thought that we ought to do something in return. So I said: "Father, should we not offer one of these to the wild things?" He looked hard at me again for a while. Then he placed one of the deer with its head to the east, and, facing the west, he raised his hand and cried, "Hey-hey" four times and prayed like this: "Grandfather, the Great Spirit, behold me! To all the wild things that eat flesh, this I have offered that my people may live and the children grow up with plenty."

That was another happy summer, for the big trouble had not come yet. We cut plenty of tepee poles up along the creeks that came down the east side of the Black Hills, and there was all we wanted to eat, for the Hills were like a big food pack for our people. Iron Bull, a little boy my age, and I had great fun fishing. We always made an offering of bait to the fish, saying: "You who are down in the water with wings of red, I offer this to you; so come hither." Then when we caught the first fish, we would put it on a forked stick and kiss it. If we did not do this, we were sure the others would know and stay away. If we caught a little fish, we would kiss it and throw it back, so that it would not go and frighten the bigger fish. I don't know whether all this helped or not, but we always got plenty of fish,

and our parents were proud of us. We tried to catch as many as we could so that people would think much of us.

There was a man by the name of Watanye who was good at spearing fish, and he had very sore lips so that he did not dare to laugh. They were cracked all around his mouth. People would try to make him laugh, but he would just walk away from them. One day he said to me: "Younger brother, I will show you how to spear fish." So we went up the creek, and there was a fish this long (to the elbow) lying in a pool. "Take the spear," Watanye said, "and strike deep, for they are always farther down than they look." I took the spear and thrust with it as hard as I could; but the clear water was much deeper than it seemed. I missed and went over head-first into the cold pool. When I scrambled out, Watanye was all doubled up, hugging his belly, and going "hunh, hunh, hunh!" Blood was running down his chin. He ran away as fast as he could, and for a long while after that, whenever he saw me coming, he would turn and run, so that he would not have to laugh again. Once I hid in a bush until he came along, just to see him run when I jumped out.

I think Watanye liked me a good deal, because he often used to take me out alone to fish or hunt, and he was always teaching me things. Also, he liked to tell me stories, mostly funny ones when he did not have sore lips. I still remember one story he told me about a young Lakota called High Horse, and what a hard time he had getting the girl he wanted. Watanye said the story happened just as he told it, and maybe it did. If it did not, it could have, just as well as not. I will tell that story now.

VI

High Horse's Courting

You know, in the old days, it was not so very easy
to get a girl when you wanted to be married. Some-
times it was hard work for a young man and he
had to stand a great deal. Say I am a young man
and I have seen a young girl who looks so beautiful
to me that I feel all sick when I think about her. I
can not just go and tell her about it and then get
married if she is willing. I have to be a very sneaky
fellow to talk to her at all, and after I have managed
to talk to her, that is only the beginning.

Probably for a long time I have been feeling sick
about a certain girl because I love her so much, but
she will not even look at me, and her parents keep
a good watch over her. But I keep feeling worse and
worse all the time; so maybe I sneak up to her tepee
in the dark and wait until she comes out. Maybe I
just wait there all night and don't get any sleep at
all and she does not come out. Then I feel sicker
than ever about her.

Maybe I hide in the brush by a spring where she
sometimes goes to get water, and when she comes
by, if nobody is looking, then I jump out and hold
her and just make her listen to me. If she likes me

56

too, I can tell that from the way she acts, for she is very bashful and maybe will not say a word or even look at me the first time. So I let her go, and then maybe I sneak around until I can see her father alone, and I tell him how many horses I can give him for his beautiful girl, and by now I am feeling so sick that maybe I would give him all the horses in the world if I had them.

Well, this young man I am telling about was called High Horse, and there was a girl in the village who looked so beautiful to him that he was just sick all over from thinking about her so much and he was getting sicker all the time. The girl was very shy, and her parents thought a great deal of her because they were not young any more and this was the only child they had. So they watched her all day long, and they fixed it so that she would be safe at night too when they were asleep. They thought so much of her that they had made a rawhide bed for her to sleep in, and after they knew that High Horse was sneaking around after her, they took rawhide thongs and tied the girl in bed at night so that nobody could steal her when they were asleep, for they were not sure but that their girl might really want to be stolen.

Well, after High Horse had been sneaking around a good while and hiding and waiting for the girl and getting sicker all the time, he finally caught her alone and made her talk to him. Then he found out that she liked him maybe a little. Of course this did not make him feel well. It made him sicker than ever, but now he felt as brave as a bison bull, and so he went right to her father and said he loved the girl so much that he would give two good horses for her—one of them young and the other one not so very old.

57

But the old man just waved his hand, meaning for High Horse to go away and quit talking foolishness like that.

High Horse was feeling sicker than ever about it; but there was another young fellow who said he would loan High Horse two ponies and when he got some more horses, why, he could just give them back for the ones he had borrowed.

Then High Horse went back to the old man and said he would give four horses for the girl—two of them young and the other two not hardly old at all. But the old man just waved his hand and would not say anything.

So High Horse sneaked around until he could talk to the girl again, and he asked her to run away with him. He told her he thought he would just fall over and die if she did not. But she said she would not do that; she wanted to be bought like a fine woman. You see she thought a great deal of herself too.

That made High Horse feel so very sick that he could not eat a bite, and he went around with his head hanging down as though he might just fall down and die any time.

Red Deer was another young fellow, and he and High Horse were great comrades, always doing things together. Red Deer saw how High Horse was acting, and he said: "Cousin, what is the matter? Are you sick in the belly? You look as though you were going to die."

Then High Horse told Red Deer how it was, and said he thought he could not stay alive much longer if he could not marry the girl pretty quick.

Red Deer thought awhile about it, and then he said: "Cousin, I have a plan, and if you are man

enough to do as I tell you, then everything will be all right. She will not run away with you; her old man will not take four horses; and four horses are all you can get. You must steal her and run away with her. Then afterwhile you can come back and the old man cannot do anything because she will be your woman. Probably she wants you to steal her anyway."

So they planned what High Horse had to do, and he said he loved the girl so much that he was man enough to do anything Red Deer or anybody else could think up.

So this is what they did.

That night late they sneaked up to the girl's tepee and waited until it sounded inside as though the old man and the old woman and the girl were sound asleep. Then High Horse crawled under the tepee with a knife. He had to cut the rawhide thongs first, and then Red Deer, who was pulling up the stakes around that side of the tepee, was going to help drag the girl outside and gag her. After that, High Horse could put her across his pony in front of him and hurry out of there and be happy all the rest of his life.

When High Horse had crawled inside, he felt so nervous that he could hear his heart drumming, and it seemed so loud he felt sure it would 'waken the old folks. But it did not, and afterwhile he began cutting the thongs. Every time he cut one it made a pop and nearly scared him to death. But he was getting along all right and all the thongs were cut down as far as the girl's thighs, when he became so nervous that his knife slipped and stuck the girl. She gave a big, loud yell. Then the old folks jumped up and yelled too. By this time High Horse was outside,

and he and Red Deer were running away like ante-
lope. The old man and some other people chased
the young men but they got away in the dark and
nobody knew who it was.

Well, if you ever wanted a beautiful girl you will
know how sick High Horse was now. It was very
bad the way he felt, and it looked as though he
would starve even if he did not drop over dead some-
time.

Red Deer kept thinking about this, and after a
few days he went to High Horse and said: "Cousin,
take courage! I have another plan, and I am sure,
if you are man enough, we can steal her this time."
And High Horse said: "I am man enough to do
anything anybody can think up, if I can only get
that girl."

So this is what they did.

They went away from the village alone, and Red
Deer made High Horse strip naked. Then he painted
High Horse solid white all over, and after that he
painted black stripes all over the white and put black
rings around High Horse's eyes. High Horse looked
terrible. He looked so terrible that when Red Deer
was through painting and took a good look at what
he had done, he said it scared even him a little.

"Now," Red Deer said, "if you get caught again,
everybody will be so scared they will think you are
a bad spirit and will be afraid to chase you."

So when the night was getting old and everybody
was sound asleep, they sneaked back to the girl's
tepee. High Horse crawled in with his knife, as be-
fore, and Red Deer waited outside, ready to drag the
girl out and gag her when High Horse had all the
thongs cut.

High Horse crept up by the girl's bed and began

cutting at the thongs. But he kept thinking, "If they see me they will shoot me because I look so terrible." The girl was restless and kept squirming around in bed, and when a thong was cut, it popped. So High Horse worked very slowly and carefully.

But he must have made some noise, for suddenly the old woman awoke and said to her old man: "Old Man, wake up! There is somebody in this tepee!" But the old man was sleepy and didn't want to be bothered. He said: "Of course there is somebody in this tepee. Go to sleep and don't bother me." Then he snored some more.

But High Horse was so scared by now that he lay very still and as flat to the ground as he could. Now, you see, he had not been sleeping very well for a long time because he was so sick about the girl. And while he was lying there waiting for the old woman to snore, he just forgot everything, even how beautiful the girl was. Red Deer, who was lying outside ready to do his part, wondered and wondered what had happened in there, but he did not dare call out to High Horse.

Afterwhile the day began to break and Red Deer had to leave with the two ponies he had staked there for his comrade and girl, or somebody would see him.

So he left.

Now when it was getting light in the tepee, the girl awoke and the first thing she saw was a terrible animal, all white with black stripes on it, lying asleep beside her bed. So she screamed, and then the old woman screamed and the old man yelled. High Horse jumped up, scared almost to death, and he nearly knocked the tepee down getting out of there.

People were coming running from all over the

village with guns and bows and axes, and everybody was yelling.

By now High Horse was running so fast that he hardly touched the ground at all, and he looked so terrible that the people fled from him and let him run. Some braves wanted to shoot at him, but the others said he might be some sacred being and it would bring bad trouble to kill him.

High Horse made for the river that was near, and in among the brush he found a hollow tree and dived into it. Afterwhile some braves came there and he could hear them saying that it was some bad spirit that had come out of the water and gone back in again.

That morning the people were ordered to break camp and move away from there. So they did, while High Horse was hiding in his hollow tree.

Now Red Deer had been watching all this from his own tepee and trying to look as though he were as much surprised and scared as all the others. So when the camp moved, he sneaked back to where he had seen his comrade disappear. When he was down there in the brush, he called, and High Horse answered, because he knew his friend's voice. They washed off the paint from High Horse and sat down on the river bank to talk about their troubles.

High Horse said he never would go back to the village as long as he lived and he did not care what happened to him now. He said he was going to go on the war-path all by himself. Red Deer said: "No, cousin, you are not going on the war-path alone, because I am going with you."

So Red Deer got everything ready, and at night they started out on the war-path all alone. After several days they came to a Crow camp just about

sundown, and when it was dark they sneaked up to where the Crow horses were grazing, killed the horse guard, who was not thinking about enemies because he thought all the Lakotas were far away, and drove off about a hundred horses.

They got a big start because all the Crow horses stampeded and it was probably morning before the Crow warriors could catch any horses to ride. Red Deer and High Horse fled with their herd three days and nights before they reached the village of their people. Then they drove the whole herd right into the village and up in front of the girl's tepee. The old man was there, and High Horse called out to him and asked if he thought maybe that would be enough horses for his girl. The old man did not wave him away that time. It was not the horses that he wanted. What he wanted was a son who was a real man and good for something.

So High Horse got his girl after all, and I think he deserved her.

VII

Wasichus in the Hills

It was the next summer, when I was 11 years old (1874), that the first sign of a new trouble came to us. Our band had been camping on Split-Toe Creek in the Black Hills, and from there we moved to Spring Creek, then to Rapid Creek where it comes out into the prairie. That evening, just before sunset, a big thunder cloud came up from the west, and just before the wind struck, there were clouds of split-tail swallows flying all around above us. It was like a part of my vision, and it made me feel queer. The boys tried to hit the swallows with stones and it hurt me to see them doing this, but I could not tell them. I got a stone and acted as though I were going to throw, but I did not. The swallows seemed holy. Nobody hit one, and when I thought about this I knew that of course they could not.

The next day some of the people were building a sweat tepee for a medicine man by the name of Chips, who was going to perform a ceremony and had to be purified first. They say he was the first man who made a sacred ornament for our great chief, Crazy Horse. While they were heating the stones for the sweat tepee, some boys asked me to

go with them to shoot squirrels. We went out, and when I was about to shoot at one, I felt very uneasy all at once. So I sat down, feeling queer, and wondered about it. While I sat there I heard a voice that said: "Go at once! Go home!" I told the boys we must go home at once, and we all hurried. When we got back, everybody was excited, breaking camp, catching the ponies and loading the drags; and I heard that while Chips was in the sweat tepee a voice had told him that the band must flee at once because something was going to happen there.

It was nearly sundown when we started, and we fled all that night on the back trail toward Spring Creek, then down that creek to the south fork of the Good River. I rode most of the night in a pony drag because I got too sleepy to stay on a horse. We camped at Good River in the morning, but we stayed only long enough to eat. Then we fled again, upstream, all day long until we reached the mouth of Horse Creek. We were going to stay there, but scouts came to us and said that many soldiers had come into the Black Hills; and that was what Chips saw while he was in the sweat tepee. So we hurried on in the night towards Smoky Earth River (the White), and when we got there, I woke up and it was daybreak. We camped a while to eat, and then went up the Smoky Earth, two camps, to Robinson, for we were afraid of the soldiers up there.

Afterward I learned that it was Pahuska[1] who had led his soldiers into the Black Hills that summer to see what he could find. He had no right to go in there, because all that country was ours. Also the Wasichus had made a treaty with Red Cloud

[1] Long Hair, General Custer.

(1868) that said it would be ours as long as grass should grow and water flow. Later I learned too that Pahuska had found there much of the yellow metal that makes the Wasichus crazy; and that is what made the bad trouble, just as it did before, when the hundred were rubbed out.

Our people knew there was yellow metal in little chunks up there; but they did not bother with it, because it was not good for anything.

We stayed all winter at the Soldiers' Town, and all the while the bad trouble was coming fast; for in the fall we heard that some Wasichus had come from the Missouri River to dig in the Black Hills for the yellow metal, because Pahuska had told about it with a voice that went everywhere. Later he got rubbed out for doing that.

The people talked about this all winter. Crazy Horse was in the Powder River country and Sitting Bull was somewhere north of the Hills. Our people at the Soldiers' Town thought we ought to get together and do something. Red Cloud's people said that the soldiers had gone in there to keep the diggers out, but we, who were only visiting, did not believe it. We called Red Cloud's people "Hangs-Around-The-Fort," and our people said they were standing up for the Wasichus, and if we did not do something we should lose the Black Hills.

In the spring when I was twelve years old (1875), more soldiers with many wagons came up from the Soldiers' Town at the mouth of the Laramie River[2] and went into the Hills.

There was much talk all summer, and in the

2 Colonel Dodge with 400 men and 75 wagons from Fort Laramie escorted a geological expedition into the Hills that spring and remained until October.

Moon of Making Fat (June) there was a sun dance there at the Soldiers' Town to give the people strength, but not many took part; maybe because everybody was so excited talking about the Black Hills. I remember two men who danced together. One had lost a leg in the Battle of the Hundred Slain and one had lost an eye in the Attacking of the Wagons, so they had only three eyes and three legs between them to dance with. We boys went down to the creek while they were sun dancing and got some elm leaves that we chewed up and threw on the dancers while they were all dressed up and trying to look their best. We even did this to some of the older people, and nobody got angry, because everybody was supposed to be in a good humor and to show their endurance in every kind of way; so they had to stand teasing too. I will tell about a big sun dance later when we come to it.

In the Moon When the Calves Grow Hair (September) there was a big council with the Wasichus on the Smoky Earth River at the mouth of White Clay Creek. I can remember the council, but I did not understand much of it then. Many of the Lakotas were there, also Shyelas and Blue Clouds[3]; but Crazy Horse and Sitting Bull stayed away. In the middle of the circle there was a shade made of canvas. Under this the councilors sat and talked, and all around them there was a crowd of people on foot and horseback. They talked and talked for days, but it was just like wind blowing in the end. I asked my father what they were talking about in there, and he told me that the Grandfather at Washington wanted to lease the Black Hills so that the

[3] Cheyennes and Arapahoes.

67

Wasichus could dig yellow metal, and that the chief
of the soldiers had said if we did not do this, the
Black Hills would be just like melting snow held in
our hands, because the Wasichus would take that
country anyway.

It made me sad to hear this. It was such a good
place to play and the people were always happy in
that country. Also I thought of my vision, and of how
the spirits took me there to the center of the world.

After the council we heard that creeks of Wasi-
chus were flowing into the Hills and becoming
rivers, and that they were already making towns up
there. It looked like bad trouble coming, so our band
broke camp and started out to join Crazy Horse on
Powder River. We camped on Horsehead Creek, then
on the War Bonnet after we crossed the old Wasichu's
road[4] that made the trouble that time when the
hundred were rubbed out. Grass was growing on it.
Then we camped at Sage Creek, then on the Beaver,
then on Driftwood Creek, and came again to the
Plain of Pine Trees at the edge of the Hills.

The nights were sharp now, but the days were
clear and still; and while we were camping there I
went up into the Hills alone and sat a long while
under a tree. I thought maybe my vision would
come back and tell me how I could save that coun-
try for my people, but I could not see anything clear.

This made me sad, but something happened a
few days later that made me feel good. We had
gone over to Taking-The-Crow-Horses Creek, where
we found many bison and made plenty of meat and
tanned many hides for winter. In our band there
was a man by the name of Fat, who was always

[4] The Bozeman Trail.

talking about how fast his horse could run. One day while we were camping there I told Fat my pony could run faster than his could, and he laughed at me and said that only crows and coyotes would think my pony was any good. I asked him what he would give me if my pony could beat his, and he said he would give me some black medicine (coffee). So we ran, and I got the black medicine. All the while we were running I thought about the white wing of the wind that the Second Grandfather of my vision gave me; and maybe that power went into my pony's legs.

On Kills-Himself Creek we made more meat and hides and were ready to join Crazy Horse's camp on the Powder. There were some Hang-Around-The-Fort people with us, and when they saw that we were going to join Crazy Horse, they left us and started back to the Soldiers' Town. They were afraid there might be trouble, and they knew Crazy Horse would fight, so they wanted to be safe with the Wasichus. We did not like them very much.

We had no advisers, because we were just a little band, and when we were moving, the boys could ride anywhere. One day while we were heading for Powder River I was riding ahead with Steals Horses, another boy my age, and we saw some footprints of somebody going somewhere. We followed the footprints and there was a knoll beside a creek where a Lakota was lying. We got off and looked at him, and he was dead. His name was Root-of-the-Tail, and he was going over to Tongue River to see his relatives when he died. He was very old and ready to die, so he just lay down and died right there before he saw his relatives again.

Afterwhile we came to the village on Powder

River and went into camp at the downstream end. I was anxious to see my cousin, Crazy Horse, again, for now that it began to look like bad trouble coming, everybody talked about him more than ever and he seemed greater than before. Also I was getting older.

Of course I had seen him now and then ever since I could remember, and had heard stories of the brave things he did. I remember the story of how he and his brother were out alone on horseback, and a big band of Crows attacked them, so that they had to run. And while they were riding hard, with all those Crows after them, Crazy Horse heard his brother call out; and when he looked back, his brother's horse was down and the Crows were almost on him. And they told how Crazy Horse charged back right into the Crows and fought them back with only a bow and arrows, then took his brother up behind him and got away. It was his sacred power that made the Crows afraid of him when he charged. And the people told stories of when he was a boy and used to be around with the older Hump all the time. Hump was not young any more at the time, and he was a very great warrior, maybe the greatest we ever had until then. They say people used to wonder at the boy and the old man always being together; but I think Hump knew Crazy Horse would be a great man and wanted to teach him everything.

Crazy Horse's father was my father's cousin, and there were no chiefs in our family before Crazy Horse; but there were holy men; and he became a chief bcause of the power he got in a vision when he was a boy. When I was a man, my father told me something about that vision. Of course he did not know all of it; but he said that Crazy Horse

dreamed and went into the world where there is nothing but the spirits of all things. That is the real world that is behind this one, and everything we see here is something like a shadow from that world. He was on his horse in that world, and the horse and himself on it and the trees and the grass and the stones and everything were made of spirit, and nothing was hard, and everything seemed to float. His horse was standing still there, and yet it danced around like a horse made only of shadow, and that is how he got his name, which does not mean that his horse was crazy or wild, but that in his vision it danced around in that queer way.

It was this vision that gave him his great power, for when he went into a fight, he had only to think of that world to be in it again, so that he could go through anything and not be hurt. Until he was murdered by the Wasichus at the Soldiers' Town on White River, he was wounded only twice, once by accident and both times by some one of his own people when he was not expecting trouble and was not thinking; never by an enemy. He was fifteen years old when he was wounded by accident; and the other time was when he was a young man and another man was jealous of him because the man's wife liked Crazy Horse.

They used to say too that he carried a sacred stone with him, like one he had seen in some vision, and that when he was in danger, the stone always got very heavy and protected him somehow. That, they used to say, was the reason no horse he ever rode lasted very long. I do not know about this; maybe people only thought it; but it is a fact that he never kept one horse long. They wore out. I

71

think it was only the power of his great vision that made him great.

Now and then he would notice me and speak to me before this; and sometimes he would have the crier call me into his tepee to eat with him. Then he would say things to tease me, but I would not say anything back, because I think I was a little afraid of him. I was not afraid that he would hurt me; I was just afraid. Everybody felt that way about him, for he was a queer man and would go about the village without noticing people or saying anything. In his own tepee he would joke, and when he was on the warpath with a small party, he would joke to make his warriors feel good. But around the village he hardly ever noticed anybody, except little children. All the Lakotas like to dance and sing; but he never joined a dance, and they say nobody ever heard him sing. But everybody liked him, and they would do anything he wanted or go anywhere he said. He was a small man among the Lakotas and he was slender and had a thin face and his eyes looked through things and he always seemed to be thinking hard about something. He never wanted to have many things for himself, and did not have many ponies like a chief. They say that when game was scarce and the people were hungry, he would not eat at all. He was a queer man. Maybe he was always part way into that world of his vision. He was a very great man, and I think if the Wasichus had not murdered him down there, maybe we should still have the Black Hills and be happy. They could not have killed him in battle. They had to lie to him and murder him. And he was only about thirty years old when he died.

One day after we had camped there on Powder

River, I went upstream to see him again, but his tepee was empty and he was gone somewhere, maybe with a war-party against the Crows, for we were close to them now and had to look out for them all the time. Later I did see him. He put his arm across my shoulder and took me into his tepee and we sat down together. I do not remember what he said, but I know he did not say much, and he did not tease me. Maybe he was thinking about the trouble coming.

We did not stay together there very long, but scattered out and camped in different places so that the people and the ponies would all have plenty. Crazy Horse kept his village on Powder River with about a hundred tepees, and our band made camp on the Tongue. We built a corral of poles for the horses at night and herded them all day, because the Crows were great horse-thieves and we had to be careful. The women chopped and stripped cottonwood trees during the day and gave the bark to the horses at night. The horses liked it and it made them sleek and fat.

Beside the mouth of the corral there was a tepee for the horse guard, and one night Crow Nose was staying there and his wife was with him. He had a hole in the tepee so that he could look through. Afterwhile he got very sleepy, so he woke his wife and told her to get up and watch while he had a little rest. By and by she saw something dark moving slowly on the snow out there, so she woke her husband and whispered, "Old man, you'd better get up, for I think I see something." So Crow Nose got up and peeped out and saw a man moving around the corral in the starlight looking for the best horse. Crow Nose told his wife to keep her eye

at the hole and let him know when the man was coming out with a horse, and he lay down at the opening of the tepee with the muzzle of his gun sticking out of the flap. By and by they could hear the bar lifted at the mouth of the corral. When his wife touched him, Crow Nose thrust his head outside and saw the man just getting on a horse to ride away. He was black against the sky, so Crow Nose shot him, and the shot woke the whole camp so that many came running with guns and coup sticks. Yellow Shirt was the first to count coup[5] on the dead Crow, but many followed. A man who has killed an enemy must not touch him, for he has already had the honor of killing. He must let another count coup. When I got there to see, a pile of coup sticks was lying beside the Crow and the women had cut him up with axes and scattered him around. It was horrible. Then the people built a fire right there beside the Crow and we had a kill dance. Men, women, and children danced right in the middle of the night, and they sang songs about Crow Nose who had killed and Yellow Shirt who had counted the first coup.

Then it was daylight, and the crier told us we would move camp to the place where Root-of-the-Tail died. Crow Nose dressed up for war, painted his face black and rode the horse the enemy had tried to steal. When the men paint their faces black, the women all rejoice and make the tremolo, because it means their men are going to kill enemies.

When we camped again, one of Red Cloud's loafers who had started back for the Soldiers' Town because

[5] The act of striking an enemy, dead or alive, with a stick conferred distinction, the first coup naturally counting most.

they were afraid there might be trouble, came in and said the Crows had killed all his party but himself, while they were sleeping, and he had escaped because he was out scouting.

During the winter, runners came from the Wasichus and told us we must come into the Soldiers' Town right away or there would be bad trouble. But it was foolish to say that, because it was very cold and many of our people and ponies would have died in the snow. Also, we were in our own country and were doing no harm.

Late in the Moon of the Dark Red Calves (February) there was a big thaw, and our little band started for the Soldiers' Town, but it was very cold again before we got there. Crazy Horse stayed with about a hundred tepees on Powder, and in the middle of the Moon of the Snowblind (March) something bad happened there. It was just daybreak. There was a blizzard and it was very cold. The people were sleeping. Suddenly there were many shots and horses galloping through the village. It was the cavalry of the Wasichus, and they were yelling and shooting and riding their horses against the tepees. All the people rushed out and ran, because they were not awake yet and they were frightened. The soldiers killed as many women and children and men as they could while the people were running toward a bluff. Then they set fire to some of the tepees and knocked the others down. But when the people were on the side of the bluff, Crazy Horse said something, and all the warriors began singing the death song and charged back upon the soldiers; and the soldiers ran, driving many of the people's ponies ahead of them. Crazy Horse followed them all that day with a band of warriors, and that night

he took all the stolen ponies away from them, and some of their own horses, and brought them all back to the village.[6]

These people were in their own country and were doing no harm. They only wanted to be let alone. We did not hear of this until quite awhile afterward; but at the Soldiers' Town we heard enough to make us paint our faces black.

[6] Colonel Reynolds with six companies of cavalry attacked Crazy Horse's village as stated in the early morning of March 16, 1876.

VIII

The Fight with Three Stars

We stayed at the Soldiers' Town this time until the grass was good in the Moon When the Ponies Shed (May). Then my father told me we were going back to Crazy Horse and that we were going to have to fight from then on, because there was no other way to keep our country. He said that Red Cloud was a cheap man and wanted to sell the Black Hills to the Wasichus; that Spotted Tail and other chiefs were cheap men too, and that the Hang-Around-the-Fort people were all cheap and would stand up for the Wasichus. My aunt, who was living at the Soldiers' Town, must have felt the way we did, because when we were breaking camp she gave me a six-shooter like the soldiers had, and told me I was a man now. I was thirteen years old and not very big for my age, but I thought I should have to be a man anyway. We boys had practiced endurance, and we were all good riders, and I could shoot straight with either a bow or a gun.

We were a small band, and we started in the night and traveled fast. Before we got to War Bonnet Creek, some Shyelas (Cheyennes) joined us, because their hearts were bad like ours and they were going

to the same place. Later I learned that many small
bands were doing the same thing and coming to-
gether from everywhere.

Just after we camped on the War Bonnet, our
scouts saw a wagon train of the Wasichus coming
up the old road that caused the trouble before.[1]
They had oxen hitched to their wagons and they
were part of the river of Wasichus that was running
into the Black Hills. They shot at our scouts, and
we decided we would attack them. When the war
party was getting ready, I made up my mind that,
small as I was, I might as well die there, and if I
did, maybe I'd be known. I told Jumping Horse, a
boy about my age, that I was going along to die,
and he said he would too. So we went, and so did
Crab and some other boys.

When the Wasichus saw us coming, they put
their wagons in a circle and got inside with their
oxen. We rode around and around them in a wide
circle that kept getting narrower. That is the best
way to fight, because it is hard to hit ponies running
fast in a circle. And sometimes there would be two
circles, one inside the other, going fast in opposite
directions, which made us still harder to hit. The
cavalry of the Wasichus did not know how to fight.
They kept together, and when they came on, you
could hardly miss them. We kept apart in the circle.
While we were riding around the wagons, we were
hanging low on the outside of the ponies and shoot-
ing under their necks. This was not easy to do, even
when your legs were long, and mine were not yet
very long. But I stuck tight and shot with the six-
shooter my aunt gave me. Before we started the at-

[1] The Bozeman Trail, closed by the Treaty of 1868.

tack I was afraid, but Big Man told us we were brave boys, and I soon got over being frightened. The Wasichus shot fast at us from behind the wagons, and I could hear bullets whizzing, but they did not hit any of us. I kept thinking of my vision, and maybe that helped. I do not know whether we killed any Wasichus or not. We rode around several times, and once we got close, but there were not many of us and we could not get at the Wasichus behind their wagons; so we went away. This was my first fight. When we were going back to camp, some Shyela warriors told us we were very brave boys, and that we were going to have plenty of fighting.

We were traveling very fast now, for we were in danger and wanted to get back to Crazy Horse. He had moved over west to the Rosebud River, and the people were gathering there. As we traveled, we met other little bands all going to the same place, until there were a good many of us all mixed up before we got there. Red Cloud's son was with us, but Red Cloud stayed at the Soldiers' Town.

When we came to the ridge on this side of the Rosebud River, we could see the valley full of tepees, and the ponies could not be counted. Many, many people were there—Ogalalas, Hunkpapas, Minneconjous, Sans Arcs, Black Feet, Brules, Santees, and Yanktonais; also many Shyelas and Blue Clouds had come to fight with us. The village was long, and you could not see all the camps with one look. The scouts came out to meet us and bring us in, and everybody rejoiced that we had come. Great men were there: Crazy Horse and Big Road of the Ogalalas; Sitting Bull and Gall and Black Moon and Crow King of the Hunkpapas; Spotted Eagle of the Sans Arcs; the younger Hump and Fast Bull of the

Minneconjous; Dull Knife and Ice Bear of the
Shyelas; Inkpaduta with the Santees and Yanktonais.
Great men were there with all those people and
horses. Hetchetu aloh![2]

About the middle of the Moon of Making Fat
(June) the whole village moved a little way up
the River to a good place for a sun dance. The
valley was wide and flat there, and we camped in
a great oval with the river flowing through it, and
in the center they built the bower of branches in a
circle for the dancers, with the opening of it to the
east whence comes the light. Scouts were sent out in
all directions to guard the sacred place. Sitting
Bull, who was the greatest medicine man of the na-
tion at that time, had charge of this dance to purify
the people and to give them power and endurance.
It was held in the Moon of Fatness because that is
the time when the sun is highest and the growing
power of the world is strongest. I will tell you how
it was done.

First a holy man was sent out all alone to find
the waga chun,[3] the holy tree that should stand in
the middle of the dancing circle. Nobody dared fol-
low to see what he did or hear the sacred words he
would say there. And when he had found the right
tree, he would tell the people, and they would come
there singing, with flowers all over them. Then when
they had gathered about the holy tree, some women
who were bearing children would dance around it,
because the Spirit of the Sun loves all fruitfulness.
After that a warrior, who had done some very brave
deed that summer, struck the tree, counting coup

[2] It is so indeed.

[3] Rustling tree, cottonwood.

upon it; and when he had done this, he had to give gifts to those who had least of everything, and the braver he was, the more he gave away.

After this, a band of young maidens came singing, with sharp axes in their hands; and they had to be so good that nobody there could say anything against them, or that any man had ever known them; and it was the duty of any one who knew anything bad about any of them to tell it right before all the people there and prove it. But if anybody lied, it was very bad for him.

The maidens chopped the tree down and trimmed its branches off. Then chiefs, who were the sons of chiefs, carried the sacred tree home, stopping four times on the way, once for each season, giving thanks for each.

Now when the holy tree had been brought home but was not yet set up in the center of the dancing place, mounted warriors gathered around the circle of the village, and at a signal they all charged inward upon the center where the tree would stand, each trying to be the first to touch the sacred place; and whoever was the first could not be killed in war that year. When they all came together in the middle, it was like a battle, with the ponies rearing and screaming in a big dust and the men shouting and wrestling and trying to throw each other off the horses.

After that there was a big feast and plenty for everybody to eat, and a big dance just as though we had won a victory.

The next day the tree was planted in the center by holy men who sang sacred songs and made sacred vows to the Spirit. And the next morning nursing mothers brought their holy little ones to lay them

at the bottom of the tree, so that the sons would be brave men and the daughters the mothers of brave men. The holy men pierced the ears of the little ones, and for each piercing the parents gave away a pony to some one who was in need.

The next day the dancing began, and those who were going to take part were ready, for they had been fasting and purifying themselves in the sweat lodges, and praying. First, their bodies were painted by the holy men. Then each would lie down beneath the tree as though he were dead, and the holy men would cut a place in his back or chest, so that a strip of rawhide, fastened to the top of the tree, could be pushed through the flesh and tied. Then the man would get up and dance to the drums, leaning on the rawhide strip as long as he could stand the pain or until the flesh tore loose.

We smaller boys had a good time during the two days of dancing, for we were allowed to do almost anything to tease the people, and they had to stand it. We would gather sharp spear grass, and when a man came along without a shirt, we would stick him to see if we could make him cry out, for everybody was supposed to endure everything. Also we made pop-guns out of young ash boughs and shot at the men and women to see if we could make them jump; and if they did, everybody laughed at them. The mothers carried water to their holy little ones in bladder bags, and we made little bows and arrows that we could hide under our robes so that we could steal up to the women and shoot holes in the bags. They were supposed to stand anything and not scold us when the water spurted out. We had a good time there.

Right after the sun dance was over, some of our

scouts came in from the south, and the crier went around the circle and said: "The scouts have returned and they have reported that soldiers are camping up the river. So, young warriors, take courage and get ready to meet them."

While they were all getting ready, I was getting ready too, because Crazy Horse was going to lead the warriors and I wanted to go with him; but my uncle, who thought a great deal of me, said: "Young nephew, you must not go. Look at the helpless ones. Stay home, and maybe there will be plenty of fighting right here." So the war parties went on without me. Maybe my uncle thought I was too little to do much and might get killed.

Then the crier told us to break camp, and we moved over west towards the Greasy Grass[4] and camped at the head of Spring Creek while the war parties were gone. We learned later that it was Three Stars[5] who fought with our people on the Rosebud that time.[6] He had many walking soldiers and some cavalry, and there were many Crows and Shoshones with him. They were all coming to attack us where we had the sun dance, but Crazy Horse whipped them and they went back to Goose Creek where they had all their wagons. My friend, Iron Hawk, was there that day, and he can tell you how it was.

Iron Hawk Speaks:

I am a Hunkpapa. I was fourteen years old that summer, and I was a big boy. Two war parties went out, a very large one from the south end of the

4 Little Big Horn.
5 General Crook.
6 June 17, 1876.

camp, and a small one from the north end. I went with the small one, and there were only about forty of us. The big party got there early in the morning, and when we came, they had been fighting a long while. There is a wide valley there at the bend of the river with some bluffs and hills around it, and it looked as though people were fighting all over that place. There were Crows with the soldiers, and we began fighting with some of them. It looked as though we were getting the best of them. Then the soldiers began to advance on the other side of us, and we had to retreat. We were heading for where the big party was, but the soldiers were after us, and the Crows got braver and fought harder because of the soldiers. When we got to the bend, the Crows were right among us, and it was all mixed up fighting there. I don't know whether I killed anybody or not, but I guess I did, for I was scared and fought hard, and the way it was you couldn't keep from killing somebody if you didn't get killed, and I am still alive. There was a Lakota with me by the name of Without-a-Tepee, and a big Crow pulled him right off his horse and he disappeared. Of course, me—I ran for my life, because we could not fight all those Crows and the soldiers too, and I was scared. But I was not running alone. We were all running, with the Crows after us. Then all at once we saw a band of cavalry coming right ahead of us —about thirty of them. I do not know how they got there. Maybe they were returning from a scouting trip. It looked bad for us. Then I heard voices crying in our language: "Take courage! This is a good day to die! Think of the children and the helpless at home!" So we all yelled "Hoka hey!" and charged on the cavalrymen and began shooting them off their

horses, for they turned and ran. They were running toward their big party, and I could see many people were fighting over there, but everything was all mixed up, and you could not tell what was happening. It was a pitiful, long-stretched-out battle. They fought all day. Then the Crows were on us from behind, and we turned around and charged back on them. But many soldiers were behind them, coming. So we all had to run, crying "yea-hey" because there were not enough of us. By now I was very scared, and I ran for my life. I came to a rocky place, and my pony stepped between two stones and nearly tore his hoof off.

There was a very brave Shyela by the name of Sitting Eagle. He was a friend of mine and he had been with me in the fight. When I got off my pony to look at his hoof, a single Crow was coming after me. Then I saw my friend, the Shyela, going to meet the Crow. They fought hand-to-hand, and the Crow went down. I wish I had stayed with Sitting Eagle, because then I could have been the first to coup that Crow. But another man did it.

I ran on foot, leading my horse, who was hopping on three legs. Then I saw smoke coming out of a deep gully where there was a creek. I went over to the smoke, and there were three Lakotas who had killed a bison and were having a feast right there while all the fighting was going on over the hill. They invited me, so I sat there and ate, for I was about fourteen years old and I was always hungry. We had to watch out while we ate. One of the men took some clotted blood from the bison and put it in some raw bison hide and fastened it around my pony's hoof so that I could ride.

After we had been eating there a long time, a La-

kota came up on his horse with blood and dirt all over his face, and he was angry. He said: "What are you doing here? We're fighting! All you think of is to eat! Why don't you think about the helpless ones at home? Come, make haste! We have got to stand our ground!"

I felt ashamed, so I got on my horse and we started. My horse could go better with his hoof tied up that way. We came to a ridge, and I could see all over the valley of the Rosebud where the fighting was going on. You could not tell who was getting whipped. It looked all mixed up. Some Crows attacked us there and I never got to the big party that was doing the hard fighting, but it was bad enough where I was, except when I was eating. I must have eaten a great deal, for it was evening now. Of course when we got there, they had been fighting a good while already.

We all came away when it was dark, to guard the women and children, and the enemy did not follow us. Of course I thought the Wasichus had whipped us; but I learned it was not so. It was not a finished battle because the night stopped it, but the Wasichus got whipped anyway, and did not attack our village. They went back to their wagons on Goose Creek and stayed there.

Standing Bear Speaks:

I was not in that fight. There were many who were not. The warriors came back in the dark, and everybody was so excited that nobody slept all night.

The next morning, about twenty of us young fellows started out to see where the fight had been. First we saw a dead horse without shoes. Then we saw a dead horse with shoes, and near this one was

a soldier full of arrows. We got to where the soldiers had camped after the fight, and there was a place where the ground was fresh and a big fire had been built on it. We started to dig there to see what was hidden. We got down on our hands and knees and dug in the loose ground. After a while we came to a blanket and there was a dead soldier in it, and it was tied around his legs and waist and neck. We pulled him out, and one of the men said: "This is my blanket. I have been looking for this blanket. I will have this blanket." So he took it.

Under that was another dead soldier tied up in a blanket, and then another and another under that. The fourth one was a black Wasichu (Negro). Each time somebody said, "This is my blanket," and took it. I got the fifth one, and the man inside was young, and he had a ring on his finger with a white stone in it that sparkled. I cut off the finger and I had the ring for a long time. One of our men scalped a soldier and started home with the scalp on a stick. When we got on top of the ridge we could see the soldiers of Three Stars retreating toward Goose Creek a long way off. A big dust was rising there. Then we went home.

The village stayed at the head of Spring Creek several days. Then we all broke camp and moved over to the Greasy Grass.

IX

The Rubbing Out of Long Hair

Black Elk Continues:

Crazy Horse whipped Three Stars on the Rosebud that day, and I think he could have rubbed the soldiers out there. He could have called many more warriors from the villages and he could have rubbed the soldiers out at daybreak, for they camped there in the dark after the fight.

He whipped the cavalry of Three Stars when they attacked his village on the Powder that cold morning in the Moon of the Snowblind (March). Then he moved farther west to the Rosebud; and when the soldiers came to kill us there, he whipped them and made them go back. Then he moved farther west to the valley of the Greasy Grass. We were in our own country all the time and we only wanted to be let alone. The soldiers came there to kill us, and many got rubbed out. It was our country and we did not want to have trouble.

We camped there in the valley along the south side of the Greasy Grass before the sun was straight above; and this was, I think, two days before the battle. It was a very big village and you could hardly count the tepees. Farthest up the stream toward the

south were the Hunkpapas, and the Ogalalas were next. Then came the Minneconjous, the Sans Arcs, the Blackfeet, the Shyelas; and last, the farthest toward the north, were the Santees and Yanktonais. Along the side towards the east was the Greasy Grass, with some timber along it, and it was running full from the melting of the snow in the Big Horn Mountains. If you stood on a hill you could see the mountains off to the south and west. On the other side of the river, there were bluffs and hills beyond. Some gullies came down through the bluffs. On the westward side of us were lower hills, and there we grazed our ponies and guarded them. There were so many they could not be counted.

There was a man by the name of Rattling Hawk who was shot through the hip in the fight on the Rosebud, and people thought he could not get well. But there was a medicine man by the name of Hairy Chin who cured him.

The day before the battle I had greased myself and was going to swim with some boys, when Hairy Chin called me over to Rattling Hawk's tepee, and told me he wanted me to help him. There were five other boys there, and he needed us for bears in the curing ceremony, because he had his power from a dream of the bear. He painted my body yellow, and my face too, and put a black stripe on either side of my nose from the eyes down. Then he tied my hair up to look like bear's ears, and put some eagle feathers on my head.

While he was doing this, I thought of my vision, and suddenly I seemed to be lifted clear off the ground; and while I was that way, I knew more things than I could tell, and I felt sure something

terrible was going to happen in a short time. I was frightened.

The other boys were painted all red and had real bear's ears on their heads.

Hairy Chin, who wore a real bear skin with the head on it, began to sing a song that went like this:

"At the doorway the sacred herbs are rejoicing."

And while he sang, two girls came in and stood one on either side of the wounded man; one had a cup of water and one some kind of a herb. I tried to see if the cup had all the sky in it, as it was in my vision, but I could not see it. They gave the cup and the herb to Rattling Hawk while Hairy Chin was singing. Then they gave him a red cane, and right away he stood up with it. The girls then started out of the tepee, and the wounded man followed, leaning on the sacred red stick; and we boys, who were the little bears, had to jump around him and make growling noises toward the man. And when we did this, you could see something like feathers of all colors coming out of our mouths. Then Hairy Chin came out on all fours, and he looked just like a bear to me. Then Rattling Hawk began to walk better. He was not able to fight next day, but he got well in a little while.

After the ceremony, we boys went swimming to wash the paint off, and when we got back the people were dancing and having kill talks all over the village, remembering brave deeds done in the fight with Three Stars on the Rosebud.

When it was about sundown we boys had to bring the ponies in close, and when this was done it was dark and the people were still dancing around fires

all over the village. We boys went around from one dance to another, until we got too sleepy to stay up any more.

My father 'woke me at daybreak and told me to go with him to take our horses out to graze, and when we were out there he said: "We must have a long rope on one of them, so that it will be easy to catch; then we can get the others. If anything happens, you must bring the horses back as fast as you can, and keep your eyes on the camp."

Several of us boys watched our horses together until the sun was straight above and it was getting very hot. Then we thought we would go swimming, and my cousin said he would stay with our horses till we got back. When I was greasing myself, I did not feel well; I felt queer. It seemed that something terrible was going to happen. But I went with the boys anyway. Many people were in the water now and many of the women were out west of the village digging turnips. We had been in the water quite a while when my cousin came down there with the horses to give them a drink, for it was very hot now.

Just then we heard the crier shouting in the Hunkpapa camp, which was not very far from us: "The chargers are coming! They are charging! The chargers are coming!" Then the crier of the Ogalalas shouted the same words; and we could hear the cry going from camp to camp northward clear to the Santees and Yanktonais.

Everybody was running now to catch the horses. We were lucky to have ours right there just at that time. My older brother had a sorrel, and he rode away fast toward the Hunkpapas. I had a buckskin. My father came running and said: Your brother has

gone to the Hunkpapas without his gun. Catch him and give it to him. Then come right back to me." He had my six-shooter too—the one my aunt gave me. I took the guns, jumped on my pony and caught my brother. I could see a big dust rising just beyond the Hunkpapa camp and all the Hunkpapas were running around and yelling, and many were running wet from the river. Then out of the dust came the soldiers on their big horses. They looked big and strong and tall and they were all shooting.[1] My brother took his gun and yelled for me to go back. There was brushy timber just on the other side of the Hunkpapas, and some warriors were gathering there. He made for that place, and I followed him. By now women and children were running in a crowd downstream. I looked back and saw them all running and scattering up a hillside down yonder.

When we got into the timber, a good many Hunkpapas were there already and the soldiers were shooting above us so that leaves were falling from the trees where the bullets struck. By now I could not see what was happening in the village below. It was all dust and cries and thunder; for the women and children were running there, and the warriors were coming on their ponies.

Among us there in the brush and out in the Hunkpapa camp a cry went up: "Take courage! Don't be a woman! The helpless are out of breath!" I think this was when Gall stopped the Hunkpapas, who had been running away, and turned them back.

I stayed there in the woods a little while and thought of my vision. It made me feel stronger, and

[1] This was Reno's detachment attacking from the southern end of the village.

it seemed that my people were all thunder-beings and that the soldiers would be rubbed out.

Then another great cry went up out in the dust: "Crazy Horse is coming! Crazy Horse is coming!" Off toward the west and north they were yelling "Hoka hey!" like a big wind roaring, and making the tremolo; and you could hear eagle bone whistles screaming.

The valley went darker with dust and smoke, and there were only shadows and a big noise of many cries and hoofs and guns. On the left of where I was I could hear the shod hoofs of the soldiers' horses going back into the brush and there was shooting everywhere. Then the hoofs came out of the brush, and I came out and was in among men and horses weaving in and out and going upstream, and everybody was yelling, "Hurry! Hurry!" The soldiers were running upstream and we were all mixed there in the twilight and the great noise. I did not see much; but once I saw a Lakota charge at a soldier who stayed behind and fought and was a very brave man.[2] The Lakota took the soldier's horse by the bridle, but the soldier killed him with a six-shooter. I was small and could not crowd in to where the soldiers were, so I did not kill anybody. There were so many ahead of me, and it was all dark and mixed up.

Soon the soldiers were all crowded into the river, and many Lakotas too; and I was in the water awhile. Men and horses were all mixed up and fighting in the water, and it was like hail falling in the river. Then we were out of the river, and people were stripping dead soldiers and putting the clothes

[2] Probably Captain French.

on themselves. There was a soldier on the ground and he was still kicking. A Lakota rode up and said to me: "Boy, get off and scalp him." I got off and started to do it. He had short hair and my knife was not very sharp. He ground his teeth. Then I shot him in the forehead and got his scalp.

Many of our warriors were following the soldiers up a hill on the other side of the river. Everybody else was turning back down stream, and on a hill away down yonder above the Santee camp there was a big dust, and our warriors whirling around in and out of it just like swallows, and many guns were going off.[3]

I thought I would show my mother my scalp, so I rode over toward the hill where there was a crowd of women and children. On the way down there I saw a very pretty young woman among a band of warriors about to go up to the battle on the hill, and she was singing like this:

> "Brothers, now your friends have come!
> Be brave! Be brave!
> Would you see me taken captive?"

When I rode through the Ogalala camp I saw Rattling Hawk sitting up in his tepee with a gun in his hands, and he was all alone there singing a song of regret that went like this:

> "Brothers, what are you doing that I can not
> do?"

When I got to the women on the hill they were

[3] Custer had attacked the camp at the northern end about four miles away.

all singing and making the tremolo to cheer the men fighting across the river in the dust on the hill. My mother gave a big tremolo just for me when she saw my first scalp.

I stayed there awhile with my mother and watched the big dust whirling on the hill across the river, and horses were coming out of it with empty saddles.

Standing Bear Speaks:

I am a Minneconjou, and our camp was third from the south. We got up late the morning of the fight. The women went out to dig turnips and two of my uncles went hunting. My grandmother, who was very old and feeble, and one of my uncles and I stayed in a tepee. When the sun was overhead, I went down to the river to swim, and when I came back all I had on was a shirt. My grandmother cooked some meat in the ashes and fed us. While we were eating, my uncle said: "When you have eaten, you must go to the horses right away. Something might happen." An older brother of mine and another man were herding the horses in two bunches on Muskrat Creek down stream below the Santee camp.

Before I finished eating, there was an excitement outside. Then I heard our crier saying that the chargers were coming. When we heard this, my uncle said: "I told you before that something might happen. You'd better go right away and help bring in the horses."

I crossed the Greasy Grass, which was breast deep, and got on top of Black Butte to look. On the other side of the Hunkpapas toward the south, I saw sol-

diers on horseback spreading out as they came down
a slope to the river. They crossed and came on at a
trot.[4] I started down the butte, but I was barefoot
and there was a big bed of cactus there. I had to go
slow, picking my way. A dust cloud was rising up
yonder; and then I could see that the Hunkpapas
were running, and when I looked over onto the hills
toward the south and east I saw other soldiers com-
ing there on horseback.[5] I did not go to the horses. I
went down through the cactus as fast as I could and
into the village. There were voices all over, and
everybody was shouting something and running
around. After awhile my older brother came driving
our horses, and my uncle said: "Hurry up! We shall
go forth!" I caught my gray horse and took my six-
shooter and hung my bow and arrows over my
shoulder. I had killed a red bird a few days before
and I fastened this in my hair. I had made a vow
that I would make an offering if this would keep me
from getting hurt in the next fight; and it did.

We started and went down stream to the mouth
of Muskrat Creek beyond the Santee camp. We were
going to meet the second band of soldiers.[6] By the
time we got there, they must have been fighting
on the hill already, because as we rode up east from
the mouth of Muskrat Creek we met a Lakota with
blood running out of his mouth and down over his
horse's shoulders. His name was Long Elk. There
were warriors ahead of us, the "fronters," who are
the bravest and have had most practice in war. I was

[4] He saw Reno advancing to the attack about four miles
away.

[5] Evidently Custer's detachment, coming to attack at the
northern end of the village.

[6] Custer's.

sixteen years old and I was in the rear with the less brave, and we had waited for our horses quite awhile.

Part way up we met another Lakota. He was on foot and he was bleeding and dizzy. He would get up and then he would fall down again. When we got farther up the hill, I could see the soldiers. They were off their horses, holding them by the bridles. They were ready for us and were shooting. Our people were all around the hill on every side by this time. I heard some of our men shouting: "They are gone!" And I saw that many of the soldiers' horses had broken loose and were running away. Everywhere our warriors began yelling: "Hoka hey! Hurry! Hurry!" Then we all went up, and it got dark with dust and smoke. I could see warriors flying all around me like shadows, and the noise of all those hoofs and guns and cries was so loud it seemed quiet in there and the voices seemed to be on top of the cloud. It was like a bad dream. All at once I saw a soldier right beside me, and I leaned over and knocked him down with the butt of the six-shooter. I think I had already shot it empty, but I don't remember when. The soldier fell off and was under the hoofs. There were so many of us that I think we did not need guns. Just the hoofs would have been enough.

After this we started down the hillside in formation toward the village, and there were dead men and horses scattered along there too. They were all rubbed out.

We were all crazy, and I will tell you something to show how crazy we were. There was a dead Indian lying there on his face, and someone said:

"Scalp that Ree!"[7] A man got off and scalped him; and when they turned the dead man over, it was a Shyela—one of our friends. We were all crazy.

We could see the women coming over now in a swarm and they were all making the tremolo. We waited around there awhile, and then we saw soldiers coming on a hill toward the south and east.[8] Everybody began yelling: "Hurry!" And we started for the soldiers. They ran back toward where they came from. One got killed, and many of us got off and couped him. Then we chased all the soldiers back to the hill where they were before.

They had their pack mules and horses on the inside and they had saddles and other things in front of them to hide themselves from bullets, but we surrounded them, and the hill we were on was higher and we could see them plain. We put our horses down under the hills so that they were safe. We all kept shooting at the soldiers and their horses. It was very hot, and there were some soldiers who started down the hill with kettles to get water from the river. They did not get far, and what was left of them went running back up the hill. I heard that some soldiers did get some water later, but I did not see them. Once a Lakota on the other side charged alone right up to the soldiers to show how brave he was, but they killed him, and we could not get his body.

[7] The Rees were enemies of the Sioux and Custer had Ree scouts with him.

[8] A detachment of Reno's command had set out to help Custer, and the rest of the command followed. They were driven back to the hill to which they had retreated after the disastrous fight in the valley at the southern end of the village.

By now it was nearly sundown. I had not been feeling hungry because there was the smell of blood everywhere; but now I began to feel hungry anyway. The bravest of the braves got together and talked over what we should do that night. They decided that some of us should go home and eat and bring back something for those who stayed to watch the soldiers. We could not get at the soldiers, so we were going to starve and dry them out.

I went back home with the others, and it was sundown then. At first I thought they had broken camp, but they had not. They had only gathered all the camps together in one solid village.

I did not go back to the hill with the others that night. We built fires all over the camp, and everybody was excited. I couldn't sleep because when I shut my eyes I could see all those horrible sights again. I think nobody slept.

Next morning early the crier went around and said: "The remainder of the soldiers shall die today!" So after we had eaten, we all got ready. This time I was dressed and had my moccasins and leggings on. The day before I had only a shirt. This time I had my saddle too. I was prepared to fight.

We all rode over there, and the party that had watched all night went home. We were scattered all around the soldiers, with our horses under the hill; but it was harder to hit the soldiers now, because they had been digging in the night. The day was very hot, and now and then some soldiers would start crawling down toward the river for a drink. We killed some of these, then the others would run back. Maybe some got water. I do not know. We kept shooting at each other. Once I heard some one cry

"Hey-hey!" I crawled over there, and a Lakota had been shot above the eyebrow and he was dead.

After a long while we heard that more soldiers were coming.[9] Then everybody started back home, and there the people were saying: "We will leave this and let it go!"

Then we all broke camp and started for the Big Horn Mountains.

If those soldiers had not come, we would have rubbed them all out on the hill.

Iron Hawk Speaks:

I am a Hunkpapa, and, as I told you before, I was fourteen years old. The sun was overhead and more, but I was eating my first meal that day, because I had been sleeping. While I was eating I heard the crier saying: "The chargers are coming." I jumped up and rushed out to our horses. They were grazing close to camp. I roped one, and the others stampeded, but my older brother had caught his horse already and headed the others off. When I got on my horse with the rope hitched around his nose, the soldiers were shooting up there and people were running and men and boys were catching their horses that were scared because of the shooting and yelling. I saw little children running up from the river where they had been swimming; and all the women and children were running down the valley.

Our horses stampeded down toward the Minneconjous, but we rounded them up again and brought them back. By now warriors were running toward the soldiers, and getting on the ponies, and many of

[9] General Terry was coming up river to the scene of the battle from the mouth of the Little Big Horn.

the Hunkpapas were gathering in the brush and timber near the place where the soldiers had stopped and got off their horses. I rode past a very old man who was shouting: "Boys, take courage! Would you see these little children taken away from me like dogs?"

I went into our tepee and got dressed for war as fast as I could; but I could hear bullets whizzing outside, and I was so shaky that it took me a long time to braid an eagle feather into my hair. Also, I had to hold my pony's rope all the time, and he kept jerking me and trying to get away. While I was doing this, crowds of warriors on horses were roaring by up stream, yelling: "Hoka hey!" Then I rubbed red paint all over my face and took my bow and arrows and got on my horse. I did not have a gun, only a bow and arrows.

When I was on my horse, the fight up stream seemed to be over, because everybody was starting back downstream and yelling: "It's a good day to die!" Soldiers were coming at the other end of the village, and nobody knew how many there were down there.

A man by the name of Little Bear rode up to me on a pinto horse, and he had a very pretty saddle blanket. He said: "Take courage, boy! The earth is all that lasts!" So I rode fast with him and the others downstream, and many of us Hunkpapas gathered on the east side of the river at the foot of a gulch that led back up the hill where the second soldier band[10] was. There was a very brave Shyela with us, and I heard someone say: "He is going!" I looked, and it was this Shyela. He had on a spotted

[10] Custer's.

war bonnet and a spotted robe made of some animal's skin and this was fastened with a spotted belt. He was going up the hill alone and we all followed part way. There were soldiers along the ridge up there and they were on foot holding their horses. The Shyela rode right close to them in a circle several times and all the soldiers shot at him. Then he rode back to where we had stopped at the head of the gulch. He was saying: "Ah, ah!" Someone said: "Shyela friend, what is the matter?" He began undoing his spotted belt, and when he shook it, bullets dropped out. He was very sacred and the soldiers could not hurt him. He was a fine looking man.

We stayed there awhile waiting for something and there was shooting everywhere. Then I heard a voice crying: "Now they are going, they are going!" We looked up and saw the cavalry horses stampeding. These were all gray horses.

I saw Little Bear's horse rear and race up hill toward the soldiers. When he got close, his horse was shot out from under him, and he got up limping because the bullet went through his leg; and he started hobbling back to us with the soldiers shooting at him. His brother-friend, Elk Nation, went up there on his horse and took Little Bear behind him and rode back safe with bullets striking all around him. It was his duty to go to his brother-friend even if he knew he would be killed.

By now a big cry was going up all around the soldiers up there and the warriors were coming from everywhere and it was getting dark with dust and smoke.

We saw soldiers start running down hill right towards us. Nearly all of them were afoot, and I think they were so scared that they didn't know what they

were doing. They were making their arms go as though they were running very fast, but they were only walking. Some of them shot their guns in the air. We all yelled "Hoka hey!" and charged toward them, riding all around them in the twilight that had fallen on us.

I met a soldier on horseback, and I let him have it. The arrow went through from side to side under his ribs and it stuck out on both sides. He screamed and took hold of his saddle horn and hung on, wobbling, with his head hanging down. I kept along beside him, and I took my heavy bow and struck him across the back of the neck. He fell from his saddle, and I got off and beat him to death with my bow. I kept on beating him awhile after he was dead, and every time I hit him I said "Hownh!" I was mad, because I was thinking of the women and little children running down there, all scared and out of breath. These Wasichus wanted it, and they came to get it, and we gave it to them. I did not see much more. I saw Brings Plenty kill a soldier with a war club. I saw Red Horn Buffalo fall. There was a Lakota riding along the edge of the gulch, and he was yelling to look out, that there was a soldier hiding in there. I saw him charge in and kill the soldier and begin slashing him with a knife.

Then we began to go towards the river, and the dust was lifting so that we could see the women and children coming over to us from across the river. The soldiers were all rubbed out there and scattered around.

The women swarmed up the hill and began stripping the soldiers. They were yelling and laughing and singing now. I saw something funny. Two fat old women were stripping a soldier, who was

wounded and playing dead. When they had him naked, they began to cut something off that he had, and he jumped up and began fighting with the two fat women. He was swinging one of them around, while the other was trying to stab him with her knife. After awhile, another woman rushed up and shoved her knife into him and he died really dead. It was funny to see the naked Wasichu fighting with the fat women.

By now we saw that our warriors were all charging on some soldiers that had come from the hill up river to help the second band that we had rubbed out. They ran back and we followed, chasing them up on their hill again where they had their pack mules. We could not hurt them much there, because they had been digging to hide themselves and they were lying behind saddles and other things. I was down by the river and I saw some soldiers come down there with buckets. They had no guns, just buckets. Some boys were down there, and they came out of the brush and threw mud and rocks in the soldiers' faces and chased them into the river. I guess they got enough to drink, for they are drinking yet. We killed them in the water.

Afterwhile it was nearly sundown, and I went home with many others to eat, while some others stayed to watch the soldiers on the hill. I hadn't eaten all day, because the trouble started just when I was beginning to eat my first meal.

Black Elk Continues:

After I showed my mother my first scalp, I stayed with the women awhile and they were all singing and making the tremolo. We could not see much of the battle for the big dust, but we knew there would

be no soldiers left. There were many other boys about my age and younger up there with their mothers and sisters, and they asked me to go over to the battle with them. So we got on our ponies and started. While we were riding down hill toward the river we saw gray horses with empty saddles stampeding toward the water. We rode over across the Greasy Grass to the mouth of a gulch that led up through the bluff to where the fighting was.

Before we got there, the Wasichus were all down, and most of them were dead, but some of them were still alive and kicking. Many other little boys had come up by this time, and we rode around shooting arrows into the Wasichus. There was one who was squirming around with arrows sticking in him, and I started to take his coat, but a man pushed me away and took the coat for himself. Then I saw something bright hanging on this soldier's belt, and I pulled it out. It was round and bright and yellow and very beautiful and I put it on me for a necklace. At first it ticked inside, and then it did not any more. I wore it around my neck a long time before I found out what it was and how to make it tick again.

Then the women all came over and we went to the top of the hill. Gray horses were lying dead there, and some of them were on top of dead Wasichus and dead Wasichus were on top of them. There were not many of our own dead there, because they had been picked up already; but many of our men were killed and wounded. They shot each other in the dust. I did not see Pahuska,[11] and I think nobody knew which one he was. There was a soldier who

[11] Custer.

was raising his arms and groaning. I shot an arrow into his forehead, and his arms and legs quivered. I saw some Lakotas holding another Lakota up. I went over there, and it was Chase-in-the-Morning's brother, who was called Black Wasichu. He had been shot through the right shoulder downward, and the bullet stopped in his left hip, because he was hanging on the side of his horse when he was hit. They were trying to give him some medicine. He was my cousin, and his father and my father were so angry over this, that they went and butchered a Wasichu and cut him open. The Wasichu was fat, and his meat looked good to eat, but we did not eat any.

There was a little boy, younger than I was, who asked me to scalp a soldier for him. I did, and he ran to show the scalp to his mother. While we were there, most of the warriors chased the other soldiers back to the hill where they had their pack mules. After awhile I got tired looking around. I could smell nothing but blood, and I got sick of it. So I went back home with some others. I was not sorry at all. I was a happy boy. Those Wasichus had come to kill our mothers and fathers and us, and it was our country. When I was in the brush up there by the Hunkpapas, and the first soldiers were shooting, I knew this would happen. I thought that my people were relatives to the thunder beings of my vision, and that the soldiers were very foolish to do this.

Everybody was up all night in the village. Next morning another war party went up to the hill where the other soldiers were, and the men who had been watching there all night came home. My mother and I went along. She rode a mare with a little colt tied beside her and it trotted along with its mother.

We could see the horses and pack mules up there,

but the soldiers were dug in. Beneath the hill, right on the west side of the Greasy Grass, were some bullberry bushes, and there was a big boy by the name of Round Fool who was running around the bushes. We boys asked him what he was doing that for, and he said: "There is a Wasichu in that bush." And there was. He had hidden there when the other soldiers ran to the hill-top and he had been there all night. We boys began shooting at him with arrows, and it was like chasing a rabbit. He would crawl from one side to the other while we were running around the bush shooting at him with our bows. Once he yelled "Ow." After awhile we set fire to the grass around the bushes, and he came out running. Some of our warriors killed him.

Once we went up the back of the hill, where some of our men were, and looked over. We could not see the Wasichus, who were lying in their dug-ins, but we saw the horses and pack mules, and many of them were dead. When we came down and crossed the river again, some soldiers shot at us and hit the water. Mother and I galloped back to the camp, and it was about sundown. By then our scouts had reported that more soldiers were coming up stream; so we all broke camp. Before dark we were ready and we started up the Greasy Grass, heading for Wood Louse Creek in the Big Horn Mountains. We fled all night, following the Greasy Grass. My two younger brothers and I rode in a pony-drag, and my mother put some young pups in with us. They were always trying to crawl out and I was always putting them back in, so I didn't sleep much.

By morning we reached a little dry creek and made camp and had a big feast. The meat had spots of fat in it, and I wish I had some of it right now.

When it was full day, we started again and came to Wood Louse Creek at the foot of the mountains, and camped there. A badly wounded man by the name of Three Bears had fits there, and he would keep saying: "Jeneny, jeneny." I do not know what he meant. He died, and we used to call that place the camp where Jeneny died.

That evening everybody got excited and began shouting: "The soldiers are coming!" I looked, and there they were, riding abreast right toward us. But it was some of our own men dressed in the soldiers' clothes. They were doing this for fun.

The scouts reported that the soldiers had not followed us and that everything was safe now. All over the camp there were big fires and kill dances all night long.

I will sing you some of the kill-songs that our people made up and sang that night. Some of them went like this:

"Long Hair has never returned,
 So his woman is crying, crying.
 Looking over here, she cries."

"Long Hair, guns I had none.
 You brought me many. I thank you!
 You make me laugh!"

"Long Hair, horses I had none.
 You brought me many. I thank you!
 You make me laugh!"

"Long Hair, where he lies nobody knows.
 Crying, they seek him.
 He lies over here."

108

"Let go your holy irons (guns).
You are not men enough to do any harm.
Let go your holy irons!"

After awhile I got so tired dancing that I went
to sleep on the ground right where I was.

My cousin, Black Wasichu, died that night.

X

Walking the Black Road

We stayed in that country near the Big Horn Mountains for about a moon, maybe a little more. My father told me all the fighting had not done any good, because the Hang-Around-the-Fort people were getting ready to sell the Black Hills to the Wasichu anyway, and that more soldiers were coming to fight us. He said that Three Stars was on Goose Creek and that many other soldiers were up on the Yellowstone, and that these would come together and have us between them.

Some of our people had been leaving us, a few at a time, and going in to live at the agencies the Wasichus had made. But there were many of us left, and so we started with all our ponies to get away from the soldiers.

We traveled in a very long line down the Rosebud and camped where the river flows through between high bluffs. Then we moved on down stream to where we had the big sun dance before the rubbing out of Long Hair. The soldiers had come through that way, and the holy place was all cut up with shod hoofs and made dirty with horse droppings.

A bison hunt

Custer's battle

Custer's battle

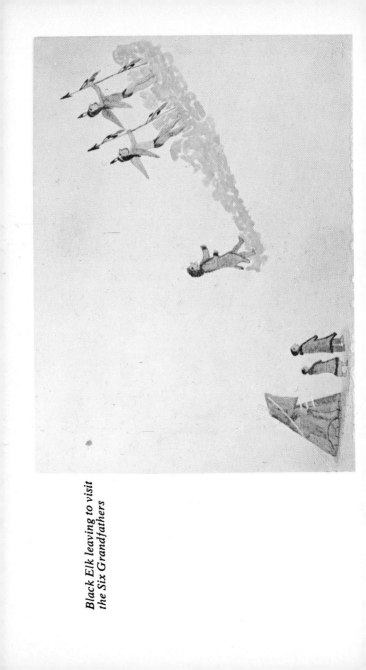

Black Elk leaving to visit the Six Grandfathers

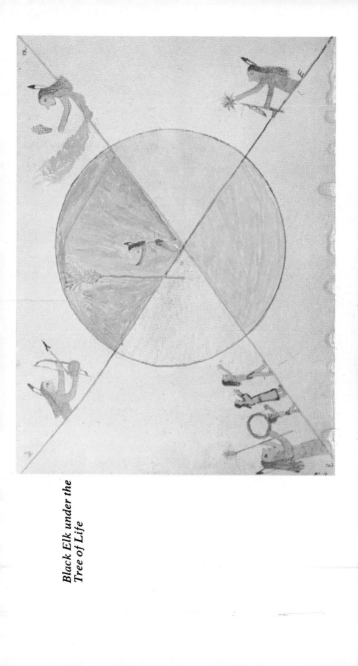

*Black Elk under the
Tree of Life*

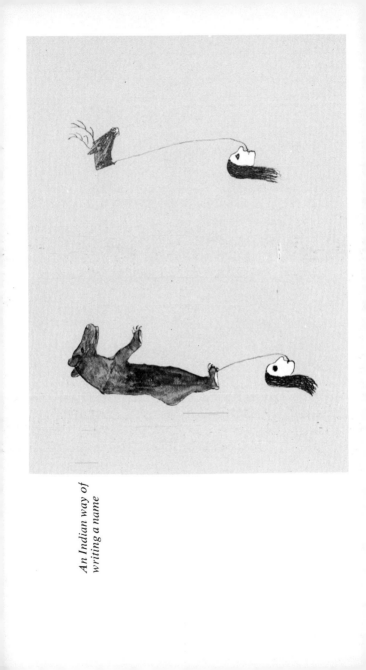

An Indian way of writing a name

Horse Dance (Chief)

*Black Elk before the
Six Grandfathers*

*Black Elk at the
center of the earth*

Killing the drought

Black Elk's spirit journey to his mother's home

*Black Elk teaching
his people the use
of the Ghost Shirt*

*U.S. soldiers
shooting Indians
at Wounded Knee*

*The massacre
at Wounded Knee*

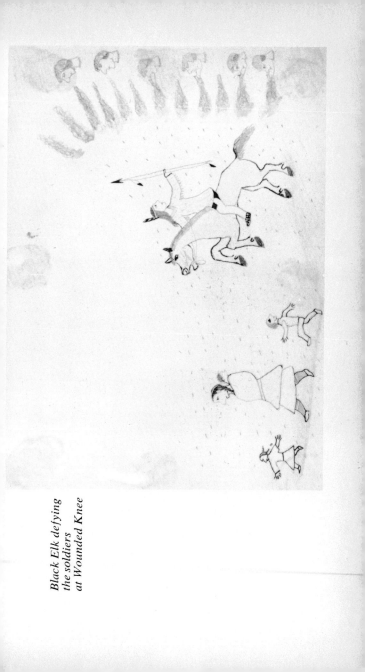

*Black Elk defying
the soldiers
at Wounded Knee*

*Black Elk at the center of
the world, Harney Peak*

Then we moved on down stream to a sacred place where there is a big rock bluff right beside the water, and high up on this bluff pictures used to appear, foretelling something important that was going to happen soon. There was a picture on it then, of many soldiers hanging head downward; and the people said it was there before the rubbing out of Long Hair. I do not know; but it was there then, and it did not seem that anybody could get up that high to make a picture.

We moved over to the Tongue River and camped a little while. When we were there, scouts came in and said that a big fire-boat[1] had come up the Yellowstone with a load of corn for the soldiers' horses, and that it was piled on the other side of the river. Some of our young men went to see, and one of them, Yellow Shirt, got killed by the fireboat's soldiers over there. But the others brought corn home and they gave us some. We parched it, and it was good.

About this time, in the Moon of Black Cherries (August), the scattering of the people began, because by now we learned that the soldiers were coming again. Dull Knife and the Shyelas went over to Willow Creek in the Big Horn Mountains. Many of the Lakotas stole away in small parties and started for the agencies. The rest of us, still a great many, started east, and the soldiers of Three Stars followed us. Our people set fire to the grass behind us as we went, and the smoke back there was wide as the day and the light of the fire was wide as the night. This was to make the soldiers' horses starve.

Then it began to rain, and it kept on raining for

[1] Steamboat.

days while we traveled east. Our ponies had to work hard in the deep mud, and it must have been bad for the soldiers' horses back there with nothing to eat.

Sitting Bull and Gall with some people left us and started for Grandmother's Land (Canada), and other people were going away from us all the time, but Crazy Horse would not leave the country that was ours.

In the Moon of the Black Calf (September) we were camping near the head of the Grand River when American Horse with many tepees had a fight with the soldiers of Three Stars by the Slim Buttes on Rabbit Creek.[2] They fought hard there in the rain, and the soldiers killed American Horse and chased the women and children out of their homes and took all the papa (dried bison meat) that they had made to feed themselves that winter. Then Crazy Horse went over there with a band of our warriors and chased the soldiers through the rain. They fled southward toward the Black Hills, and many of their horses died in the deep mud. He followed them a long way and made them fight as they fled.

Wherever we went, the soldiers came to kill us, and it was all our own country. It was ours already when the Wasichus made the treaty with Red Cloud, that said it would be ours as long as grass should grow and water flow. That was only eight winters before, and they were chasing us now because we remembered and they forgot.

After that we started west again, and we were not happy anymore, because so many of our people

[2] The Battle of Slim Buttes, September 9, 1876.

had untied their horses' tails[3] and gone over to the Wasichus. We went back deep into our country, and most of the land was black from the fire, and the bison had gone away. We camped on the Tongue River where there was some cottonwood for the ponies; and a hard winter came on early. It snowed much; game was hard to find, and it was a hungry time for us. Ponies died, and we ate them. They died because the snow froze hard and they could not find the grass that was left in the valleys and there was not enough cottonwood to feed them all. There had been thousands of us together that summer, but there were not two thousand now.

News came to us there in the Moon of the Falling Leaves (November) that the Black Hills had been sold to the Wasichus and also all the country west of the Hills—the country we were in then.[4] I learned when I was older that our people did not want to do this. The Wasichus went to some of the chiefs alone and got them to put their marks on the treaty. Maybe some of them did this when they were crazy from drinking the minne wakan (holy water, whiskey) the Wasichus gave them. I have heard this; I do not know. But only crazy or very foolish men would sell their Mother Earth. Sometimes I think it might have been better if we had stayed together and made them kill us all.

Dull Knife was camping with his band of Shyelas on Willow Creek in the edge of the Big Horn Mountains, and one morning very early near the end of the Moon of Falling Leaves the soldiers came

[3] Left the war-path.
[4] The treaty was signed in October, 1876.

there to kill them.[5] The people were all sleeping. The snow was deep and it was very cold. When the soldiers began shooting into the tepees, the people ran out into the snow, and most of them were naked from their sleeping robes. Men fought in the snow and cold with nothing on them but their cartridge belts, and it was a hard fight, because the warriors thought of the women and children freezing. They could not whip the soldiers, but those who were not killed and did not die from the cold got away and came to our camp on the Tongue.

I can remember when Dull Knife came with what was left of his starving and freezing people. They had almost nothing, and some of them had died on the way. Many little babies died. We could give them clothing, but of food we could not give them much, for we were eating ponies when they died. And afterwhile they left us and started for the Soldiers' Town on White River to surrender to the Wasichus; and so we were all alone there in that country that was ours and had been stolen from us.

After that the people noticed that Crazy Horse was queerer than ever. He hardly ever stayed in the camp. People would find him out alone in the cold, and they would ask him to come home with them. He would not come, but sometimes he would tell the people what to do. People wondered if he ate anything at all. Once my father found him out alone like that, and he said to my father: "Uncle, you have noticed me the way I act. But do not worry; there are caves and holes for me to live in,

[5] Colonel Mackenzie attacked the Cheyenne village as stated on November 26, 1876.

and out here the spirits may help me. I am making plans for the good of my people."

He was always a queer man, but that winter he was queerer than ever. Maybe he had seen that he would soon be dead and was thinking how to help us when he would not be with us any more.

It was a very bad winter for us and we were all sad. Then another trouble came. We had sent out scouts to learn where the soldiers were, and they were camping at the mouth of the Tongue. Early in the Moon of Frost in the Tepee (January), some of our scouts came in and said that the soldiers were coming up the Tongue to fight us, and that they had two wagon guns (cannon) with them.

There was no better place to go, so we got ready to fight them; and I was afraid, because my father told me we had not much ammunition left. We moved the village a little way off up stream, and our warriors were ready on a high bluff when the walking soldiers and their wagons came in the morning.[6] The soldiers built fires and ate their breakfast there in the valley while our people watched them and were hungry. Then they began shooting with the wagon guns that shot twice, because the iron balls went off after they fell. Some of them did not go off, and we boys ran after one of these and got it.

Then the walking soldiers started up the bluff, and it began to snow hard and they fought in the blizzard. We could not stop the soldiers coming up, because we had not much ammunition. The soldiers had everything. But our men used spears and guns for clubs when the soldiers got there, and they fought

[6] General Miles attacked the village of Crazy Horse on the Tongue River, January 8, 1877.

hand to hand awhile, holding the soldiers back until the women could break camp and get away with the children and ponies. We fled in the blizzard southward up the Tongue and over to the Little Powder River. The soldiers followed us awhile, and there was fighting in our rear. We got away, but we lost many things we needed, and when we camped on the Little Powder, we were almost as poor as Dull Knife's people were the day they came to us. It was so cold that the sun made himself fires, and we were eating our starving ponies.

Late in the Moon of the Dark Red Calf (February) or early in the Moon of the Snowblind (March), Spotted Tail, the Brule, with some others, came to us. His sister was Crazy Horse's mother. He was a great chief and a great warrior before he went over to the Wasichus. I saw him and I did not like him. He was fat with Wasichu food and we were lean with famine. My father told me that he came to make his nephew surrender to the soldiers, because our own people had turned against us, and in the spring when the grass was high enough for the horses, many soldiers would come and fight us, and many Shoshones and Crows and even Lakotas and our old friends, the Shyelas, would come against us with the Wasichus. I could not understand this, and I thought much about it. How could men get fat by being bad, and starve by being good? I thought and thought about my vision, and it made me very sad; for I wondered if maybe it was only a queer dream after all.

And then I heard that we would all go into the Soldiers' Town when the grass should appear, and that Crazy Horse had untied his pony's tail and would not fight again.

In the Moon of the Grass Appearing (April) our little band started for the Soldiers' Town ahead of the others, and it was early in the Moon When the Ponies Shed (May) that Crazy Horse came in with the rest of our people and the ponies that were only skin and bones. There were soldiers and Lakota policemen in lines all around him when he surrendered there at the Soldiers' Town. I saw him take off his war bonnet. I was not near enough to hear what he said. He did not talk loud and he said only a few words, and then he sat down.

I was fourteen years old. We had enough to eat now and we boys could play without being afraid of anything. Soldiers watched us, and sometimes my father and mother talked about our people who had gone to Grandmother's Land with Sitting Bull and Gall, and they wanted to be there. We were camped near Red Cloud's Agency, which was close to the Soldiers' Town. What happened that summer is not a story.

XI

The Killing of Crazy Horse

One night early in the Moon When the Calf Grows Hair (September) we broke camp there at Red Cloud Agency without making any noise, and started. My father told me we were going to Spotted Tail's camp, but he did not tell me why until later. We traveled most of the night and then we camped.

But when we were moving again next day, a band of Red Cloud's people overtook us and said there would be bad trouble if we did not come back right away. Some of us turned around then and went back, and soldiers sent the others back a little later; but Crazy Horse went on to his uncle's camp.

After what happened my father told me why Crazy Horse had done this. He was afraid somebody might start trouble down there where all the soldiers were, and the Wasichus had taken our guns away from us, so that we could do nothing if there was bad trouble. The Wasichus had made Spotted Tail head chief of all the Lakotas because he would do what they wanted, and Crazy Horse thought we might be safer there with his uncle. Afterwards, the Hang-Around-the-Fort people said that he was getting ready to tie up his horse's tail again and make

118

war on the Wasichus. How could he do that when
we had no guns and could not get any? It was a
story the Wasichus told, and their tongues were
forked when they told it. Our people believe they
did what they did because he was a great man and
they could not kill him in battle and he would not
make himself over into a Wasichu, as Spotted Tail
and the others did. That summer, my father told
me, the Wasichus wanted him to go to Washington
with Red Cloud and Spotted Tail and others to see
the Great Father there; but he would not go. He
told them that he did not need to go looking for his
Great Father. He said: "My Father is with me, and
there is no Great Father between me and the Great
Spirit."

In the evening of the next day after we got back
to Red Cloud's Agency, some soldiers came there
bringing Crazy Horse with them. He was riding his
horse alone a little way ahead. They did not stay
there long, but rode on over to the Soldiers' Town,
and my father and I went along with many others to
see what they were going to do.

When we got over there we could not see Crazy
Horse, because there were soldiers and Lakota
policemen all around where he was and people
crowding outside.

In just a little while I could feel that something
very bad was happening in there, and everybody
was excited all at once, and you could hear voices
buzzing all around. Then I heard a loud cry in our
own language, and it said: "Don't touch me! I am
Crazy Horse!" And suddenly something went through
all the people there like a big wind that strikes
many trees all at once. Somebody in there yelled
something else, but everybody around me was ask-

ing or telling everybody what had happened, and I heard that Crazy Horse was killed, that he was sick, that he was hurt; and I was frightened, because everything felt the way it did that day when we were going up to kill on the Greasy Grass, and it seemed we might all begin fighting right away.

Then everything got quiet, and everybody seemed to be waiting for something. Then the people began to break up and move around, and I heard that Crazy Horse had just taken sick and maybe he would be all right soon.

But it was not long until we all knew what had happened in there, because some of the people saw it happen, and I will tell you how it was.

They told Crazy Horse they would not harm him if he would go to the Soldiers' Town and have a talk with the Wasichu chief there. But they lied. They did not take him to the chief for a talk. They took him to the little prison with iron bars on the windows, for they had planned to get rid of him. And when he saw what they were doing, he turned around and took a knife out of his robe and started out against all those soldiers. Then Little Big Man, who had been his friend and was the one who told us boys that we were brave before my first fight when we attacked the wagons on War Bonnet Creek, took hold of Crazy Horse from behind and tried to get the knife away. And while they were struggling, a soldier ran a bayonet into Crazy Horse from one side at the back and he fell down and began to die. Then they picked him up and carried him into the soldier chief's office. The soldiers stood all around there and would not let anybody in and made the people go away. My father and I went back to our camp at Red Cloud Agency.

That night I heard mourning somewhere, and then there was more and more mourning, until it was all over the camp.

Crazy Horse was dead. He was brave and good and wise. He never wanted anything but to save his people, and he fought the Wasichus only when they came to kill us in our own country. He was only thirty years old. They could not kill him in battle. They had to lie to him and kill him that way.

I cried all night, and so did my father.

When it was day, Crazy Horse's father and mother brought him over to our camp in a wagon. Then they put him in a box, and I heard that they had to cut him in two because the box was not long enough. They fastened the box on a pony drag and went away alone toward the east and north. I saw the two old people going away alone with their son's body. Nobody followed them. They went all alone, and I can see them going yet. The horse that pulled the pony drag was a buckskin. Crazy Horse's father had a white-faced bay with white hind legs. His mother had a brown mare with a bay colt.

The old people never would tell where they took the body of their son. Nobody knows to-day where he lies, for the old people are dead too. Many have talked about the place, and some have said they knew where it was and would not tell, and many think it is somewhere on Bear Creek in the Badlands. I know one thing, and this is it. The old people came with the body right down Pepper Creek which is just a little way south across the hill from where we are.[1] There were two hunters who were

[1] Black Elk's log cabin is situated about two miles west of Manderson Post Office, Pine Ridge Reservation, South Dakota.

hunting along the creek there and they saw two old people coming with a pony drag, and when they told my father about this, they said a buckskin was pulling the drag that had a box on it; that the old man rode a white-faced bay with white hind legs and the old woman rode a brown mare with a bay colt. These hunters saw the old people coming down Pepper Creek, and later on they saw the old people again on White Horse Creek which is just a little way down Pepper Creek from where they were before. And the hunters said the box was not on the drag any more. So I think that maybe they hid the body somewhere on Pepper Creek over there because the hunters had seen them, and maybe they went back again at night and took the box away into the Badlands. But Crazy Horse might be lying over there just a little way from us right now on Pepper Creek across that hill yonder. I do not know.

It does not matter where his body lies, for it is grass; but where his spirit is, it will be good to be.

XII

Grandmother's Land

At the end of the Moon of Falling Leaves (October), after they had killed Crazy Horse, the Wasichus told us we must move from where we were over to the Missouri River and live there at different agencies they had made for us. One big band started with Red Cloud, and we started with another big band under Spotted Tail. These two bands were about a day's travel apart.

Our people were all sad because Crazy Horse was dead, and now they were going to pen us up in little islands and make us be like Wasichus. So before we had gone very far, some of us broke away and started for the country where we used to be happy. We traveled fast, and the soldiers did not follow us. But when our little band came to the Powder River country, it was not like it used to be, and we were not ready for the winter. So we kept on traveling north, and we went fast, because we wanted to be with our relatives under Sitting Bull and Gall in Grandmother's Land.[1]

It was very cold before we reached Clay Creek

[1] Canada.

where our relatives were; but they were glad to see us and took care of us. They had made plenty of meat, for there were many bison in that country; and it was a good winter. The soldiers could not come to kill us there.

I was fifteen years old that winter, and I thought much of my vision and wondered when my duty was to come; for the Grandfathers had shown me my people walking on the black road and how the nation's hoop would be broken and the flowering tree be withered, before I should bring the hoop together with the power that was given me, and make the holy tree to flower in the center and find the red road again. Part of this had happened already, and I wondered when my power would grow, so that the rest might be as I had seen it in my vision. But I could say nothing about this to anyone, because I was only a boy and people would think I was foolish and say: "What can you do if even Sitting Bull can do nothing?"

When the grasses appeared again we went bison hunting, and I was big enough now to hunt with the men. My uncle, Running Horse, and I were out together alone one day. I was riding a bay and leading my roan, which was very fast. My uncle was riding a roan and leading a brown horse. We came to Little River Creek and crossed it, and just then I began feeling queer and I knew something was going to happen. So I said to my uncle: "'I have a queer feeling and I think something is going to happen soon. I will watch while you kill a bison and we will make quick work of it and go." He looked at me in a strange way awhile. Then he said "How" and started after a bison. There were several grazing in the valley. I held my horses and watched. When he

had killed a fat cow, I went to help him butcher, but I held my horses while I was doing this, for I still had the queer feeling. Then I heard a voice that said: "Go at once and look!" I told Running Horse I would go to the top of the hill and see what was there. So I rode up and I saw two Lakota hunters galloping after a bison across a valley toward some bluffs. Just after they went out of sight behind a bluff, my horse began to prick up his ears and look around and sniff the air. Then I heard some fast shooting over there, then many horses' hoofs. Then I saw a band of about fifty horsebacks coming out from behind the bluff where the two hunters had disappeared. They were Crows, and afterwards we learned that they had killed the two hunters.

So my uncle and I took as much meat as we could and rode fast back to our village and told the others.

This showed that my power was growing, and I was glad.

In the Moon of Making Fat (June), Sitting Bull and Gall had a sun dance at Forest Butte, and afterwards we went hunting again. A man by the name of Iron Tail was with me this time, and we were out alone. I killed a big fat bison cow and we were butchering, when a thunder storm was coming up. Then it began to pour rain, and I heard a voice in the clouds that said: "Make haste! Before the day is out something will happen!"

Of course when I heard this I was excited and told Iron Tail I had heard a voice in the clouds and that we must hurry up and go. We left everything but the fat of the cow, and fled. When we got to the camp of our little band, we were excited and told the people we must flee. So they broke camp and

started. We came to Muddy Creek. It was still rain-
ing hard and we had trouble getting across because
the horses sank in the mud. A part of us got across,
but there was an old man with an old woman and a
beautiful daughter whose pony-drag got stuck in the
middle of the creek. Just then a big band of Crows
came charging, and there were so many of them that
we could not hold them off and we had to flee,
shooting back at them as they came after us.

There was a man called Brave Wolf who did a
very great deed there by the ford that day. He was
close to the pony-drag of the two old people and the
beautiful girl when it got stuck in the mud, so he
jumped off his horse, which was a very fast bison-
runner, and made the beautiful girl get on. Then he
stood there by the two old people and fought until all
three were killed. The girl got away on his fast horse.
My cousin, Hard-to-Hit, did a brave deed too, and
died. He charged back alone at a Crow who was
shooting at a Lakota in a bush, and he was killed.

The voice in the clouds had told the truth, and it
seemed that my power was growing stronger all the
time.

When my cousin, Hard-to-Hit, was killed, it was
my duty to protect his wife, so I did; and we got
lost from our little party in the dark. It rained all
night, and my cousin's wife cried so hard that I
had to make her quit for fear some enemy might
hear her and find us.

When we reached the big camp in the morning my
relatives began mourning for my cousin, Hard-To-
Hit. They would put their arms across each other's
shoulders and wail. They did this all day long, and
I had to do it too. I went around crying, "hownh,
hownh," and saying over and over: "My cousin—

he thought so much of me and I thought so much of him, and now he is dead. Hownh, hownh." I liked my cousin well enough, but I did not feel like crying all day. This was what I had to do, and it was hard work.

We stayed on Clay Creek in Grandmother's Land all that summer and the next winter when I was sixteen years old. That was a very cold winter. There were many blizzards, game was hard to find, and afterwhile the papa (dried meat) that we had made in the summer was all eaten. It looked as though we might starve to death if we did not find some game soon, and everybody was downhearted. Little hunting parties went out in different directions, but it is bad hunting in blizzard weather. My father and I started out alone leading our horses in the deep snow. When we got to Little River Creek we made a shelter with our bison robes against a bank of the stream and started a fire. That evening I saw a rabbit in a hollow tree, and when I chopped the tree down there were four rabbits in there. I killed them all, because the snow was so deep they could not get away. My father and I roasted them and we ate all four of them before we went to sleep, because it was hard walking in the snow and we had been empty a good while.

The wind went down that night and it was still and very cold. While I was lying there in a bison robe, a coyote began to howl not far off, and suddenly I knew it was saying something. It was not making words, but it said something plainer than words, and this was it: "Two-legged one, on the big ridge west of you there are bison; but first you shall see two more two-leggeds over there."

My father had dozed off, so I wakened him and

said: "Father, I have heard a coyote say that there are bison on the big ridge west of us, and that we shall first see two people over there. Let us get up early."

By this time my father had noticed that I had some kind of queer power, and he believed me. The wind came up again with the daylight, and we could see only a little way ahead when we started west in the morning. Before we came to the ridge, we saw two horses, dim in the blowing snow beside some bushes. They were huddled up with their tails to the wind and their heads hanging low. When we came closer, there was a bison robe shelter in the brush, and in it were an old man and a boy, very cold and hungry and discouraged. They were Lakotas and were glad to see us, but they were feeling weak, because they had been out two days and had seen nothing but snow. We camped there with them in the brush, and then we went up on the ridge afoot. There was much timber up there. We got behind the hill in a sheltered place and waited, but we could see nothing. While we were waiting, we talked about the people starving at home, and we were all sad. Now and then the snow haze would open up for a little bit and you could see quite a distance, then it would close again. While we were talking about our hungry people, suddenly the snow haze opened a little, and we saw a shaggy bull's head coming out of the blowing snow up the draw that led past us below. Then seven more appeared, and the snow haze came back and shut us in there. They could not see us, and they were drifting with the wind so that they could not smell us.

We four stood up and made vows to the four quarters of the world, saying: "Haho! haho!" Then

we got our horses from the brush on the other side of the ridge and came around to the mouth of the draw where the bison would pass as they drifted with the wind.

The two old men were to shoot first and then we two boys would follow the others horseback. Soon we saw the bison coming. The old people crept up and shot, but they were so cold, and maybe excited, that they got only one bison. They cried "Hoka!" and we boys charged after the other bison. The snow was blowing hard in the wind that sucked down the draw, and when we came near them the bison were so excited that they back-tracked and charged right past us bellowing. This broke the deep snow for our horses and it was easier to catch them. Suddenly I saw the bison I was chasing go out in a big flurry of snow, and I knew they had plunged into a snow-filled gulch, but it was too late to stop, and my horse plunged right in after them. There we were all together—four bison, my horse and I all floundering and kicking, but I managed to crawl out a little way. I had a repeating rifle that they gave me back at the camp, and I killed the four bison right there, but I had thrown my mittens away and the gun froze to my hands while I was shooting, so that I had to tear the skin to get it loose.

When I went back to the others, the other boy had killed three, so we had eight bison scattered around there in the snow. It was still morning, but it took till nearly dark for my father and the other old man to do the butchering. I could not help, because my hands were frozen. We finally got the meat all piled up in one place, and then we made a camp in a fine shelter behind a big rock with brush all

around it and plenty of wood. We had a big fire, and we tied our tanned robes on our horses and fed them plenty of cottonwood bark from the woods by the stream. The raw robes we used for the shelter. Then we had a big feast and we sang and were very happy.

The wind went down and it grew very cold, so we had to keep the fire going all night. During the night I heard a whimpering outside the shelter, and when I looked, there was a party of porcupines huddled up as close as they thought they dared to be, and they were crying because they were so cold. We did not chase them away, because we felt sorry for them.

We started afoot for camp next day with as much meat loaded on the horses as they could carry. The rest of it we cached by a big tree where it would be easy to find. We traveled all that day very slowly because the snow was deep, and all the while it seemed to be growing colder. At about sundown of the second day we reached camp, and the people were glad to see us with all that meat. Some other men went back later to bring in the meat we had cached.

The morning after we reached home I went out to look for our horses that were in a draw where there was cottonwood, and five of them had frozen to death. The cold was very bad after the wind stopped blowing.

We began to feel homesick for our own country where we used to be happy. The old people talked much about it and the good days before the trouble came. Sometimes I felt like crying when they did that.

XIII

The Compelling Fear

When the grasses were showing their tender faces again, two families of us started for our own country where we used to be happy. We had only five horses among us, because all the others had died in the cold, and we traveled on foot. It was a very rainy time. After awhile we came to All-Gone-Tree Creek. We came there in the afternoon and camped, and I thought I would take the horses out to eat where the grass was good. But when I had gone only a little way, all of a sudden the queer feeling came again, and I heard a voice that said: "Be careful and watch! Something you shall see!" The voice was so clear that I looked around to see who was there, and nobody was there. So I staked the horses right there not far from the camp, and sat down to think about it. There was a tall bluff a little way from the camp, and it had two points on it. So I went over there and climbed to one of the tops where there were some big rocks scattered around. I lay down in those rocks and looked all around, but I could see nothing, and I began to wonder if I was only queer in thinking I had heard a voice.

Then I looked over to the other point of the bluff

not far away, and there were two men crawling up toward the top on their bellies. I knew they were enemies, and I thought they were Crows; but later I learned that they were Blackfeet. I lay as flat as I could and peeped around a rock at the two men. They were so near that I could have thrown a rock over there, and I thought if I only had my gun I could kill them both. They stopped near the top, and one crawled a little farther and peeped over at our tepees in the valley where the women were having a hard time to get the fires started with wet wood. Then the first one motioned to the second, and they both looked over. I could hear them talking now, and I knew they were planning how to attack us. After a little while they crawled down backwards a short way, then got up and ran downhill and disappeared. When they were gone, I crawled to the other side of the bluff and went down. When I reached the bottom, I sat down and thought of my vision and began to pray to the spirits. I said: "Grandfathers, something may happen to me. But I will depend on the power you have given me. Hear me and help me!" Then I ran over to our tepees and told the people we must flee at once, because I had seen enemies planning to attack.

We were so small a party that we did not dare wait to take our tepees down, so we started right away and traveled very fast. We had to cross All-Gone-Tree Creek and it was bank-full and roaring with the big rains. So two of us boys swam across with rawhide ropes, which the old women fastened around them under their arms, and we pulled them across through the deep water. They nearly drowned before we could drag them out, because the water

was swift. Our horses swam across, and we went fast, with the old people on the horses.

As we fled east, a thunder cloud came from the west behind us, and I knew it was coming to protect us. I could hear the thunder beings crying "Hey hey!" to me. The cloud stood over us and did not rain much, but it was full of lightning and of voices.

We had not gone so very far, and it was growing dark, when we heard shooting behind us in the direction of our deserted camp, and we thought the enemies were shooting into the tepees, thinking that we might be in there yet.

It grew very dark, for the thunder cloud with the many voices hung over us, and we traveled fast all night. Then after awhile the cloud broke, and it was daybreak. We camped to eat and sleep.

I knew better than ever now that I really had power, for I had prayed for help from the Grandfathers and they had heard me and sent the thunder beings to hide us and watch over us while we fled.

When we had eaten and slept, we started again and came to a camp of Minneconjous. After that we traveled with our relatives to the mouth of the Poplar River and crossed over the Missouri on a fire-boat that was there. Then after we had hunted awhile, we went to the Soldiers' Town at the mouth of Tongue River and camped there with others of our people who had wandered away from the reservations into our old country.

The soldiers took our guns away from us and most of our horses, leaving us only two horses for every tepee.

There in the Moon of Making Fat we had a sun dance, and after this it seemed I could think of noth-

ing but my vision. I was sixteen years old and more, and I had not yet done anything the Grandfathers wanted me to do, but they had been helping me. I did not know how to do what they wanted me to do.

A terrible time began for me then, and I could not tell anybody, not even my father and mother. I was afraid to see a cloud coming up; and whenever one did, I could hear the thunder beings calling to me: "Behold your Grandfathers! Make haste!" I could understand the birds when they sang, and they were always saying: "It is time! It is time!" The crows in the day and the coyotes at night all called and called to me: "It is time! It is time! It is time!"

Time to do what? I did not know. Whenever I awoke before daybreak and went out of the tepee because I was afraid of the stillness when everyone was sleeping, there were many low voices talking together in the east, and the daybreak star would sing this song in the silence:

"In a sacred manner you shall walk!
Your nation shall behold you!"

I could not get along with people now, and I would take my horse and go far out from camp alone and compare everything on the earth and in the sky with my vision. Crows would see me and shout to each other as though they were making fun of me: "Behold him! Behold him!"

When the frosts began I was glad, because there would not be any more thunder storms for a long while, and I was more and more afraid of them all the time, for always there would be the voices crying: "Oo oohey! It is time! It is time!"

The fear was not so great all the while in the winter, but sometimes it was bad. Sometimes the crying of coyotes out in the cold made me so afraid that I would run out of one tepee into another, and I would do this until I was worn out and fell asleep. I wondered if maybe I was only crazy; and my father and mother worried a great deal about me. They said: "It is the strange sickness he had that time when we gave the horse to Whirlwind Chaser for curing him; and he is not cured." I could not tell them what was the matter, for then they would only think I was queerer than ever.

I was seventeen years old that winter.

When the grasses were beginning to show their tender faces again, my father and mother asked an old medicine man by the name of Black Road to come over and see what he could do for me. Black Road was in a tepee all alone with me, and he asked me to tell him if I had seen something that troubled me. By now I was so afraid of being afraid of everything that I told him about my vision, and when I was through he looked long at me and said: "Ah-h-h-h!," meaning that he was much surprised. Then he said to me: "Nephew, I know now what the trouble is! You must do what the bay horse in your vision wanted you to do. You must do your duty and perform this vision for your people upon earth. You must have the horse dance first for the people to see. Then the fear will leave you; but if you do not do this, something very bad will happen to you."

So we began to get ready for the horse dance.

135

XIV

The Horse Dance

There was a man by the name of Bear Sings, and he was very old and wise. So Black Road asked him to help, and he did.

First they sent a crier around in the morning who told the people to camp in a circle at a certain place a little way up the Tongue from where the soldiers were. They did this, and in the middle of the circle Bear Sings and Black Road set up a sacred tepee of bison hide, and on it they painted pictures from my vision. On the west side they painted a bow and a cup of water; on the north, white geese and the herb; on the east, the daybreak star and the pipe; on the south, the flowering stick and the nation's hoop. Also, they painted horses, elk, and bison. Then over the door of the sacred tepee, they painted the flaming rainbow. It took them all day to do this, and it was beautiful.

They told me I must not eat anything until the horse dance was over, and I had to purify myself in a sweat lodge with sage spread on the floor of it, and afterwards I had to wipe myself dry with sage.

That evening Black Road and Bear Sings told me

to come to the painted tepee. We were in there alone, and nobody dared come near us to listen. They asked me if I had heard any songs in my vision, and if I had I must teach the songs to them. So I sang to them all the songs that I had heard in my vision, and it took most of the night to teach these songs to them. While we were in there singing, we could hear low thunder rumbling all over the village outside, and we knew the thunder beings were glad and had come to help us.

My father and mother had been helping too by hunting up all that we should need in the dance. The next morning they had everything ready. There were four black horses to represent the west; four white horses for the north; four sorrels for the east; four buckskins for the south. For all of these, young riders had been chosen. Also there was a bay horse for me to ride, as in my vision. Four of the most beautiful maidens in the village were ready to take their part, and there were six very old men for the Grandfathers.

Now it was time to paint and dress for the dance. The four maidens and the sixteen horses all faced the sacred tepee. Black Road and Bear Sings then sang a song, and all the others sang along with them, like this:

"Father, paint the earth on me.
Father, paint the earth on me.
Father, paint the earth on me.
A nation I will make over.
A two-legged nation I will make holy.
Father, paint the earth on me."

After that the painting was done.

The four black-horse riders were painted all black with blue lightning stripes down their legs and arms and white hail spots on their hips, and there were blue streaks of lightning on the horses' legs.

The white-horse riders were painted all white with red streaks of lightning on their arms and legs, and on the legs of the horses there were streaks of red lightning, and all the white riders wore plumes of white horse hair on their heads to look like geese.

The riders of the sorrels of the east were painted all red with straight black lines of lightning on their limbs and across their breasts, and there was straight black lightning on the limbs and breasts of the horses too.

The riders of the buckskins of the south were painted all yellow and streaked with black lightning. The horses were black from the knees down, and black lightning streaks were on their upper legs and breasts.

My bay horse had bright red streaks of lightning on his limbs, and on his back a spotted eagle, outstretching, was painted where I sat. I was painted red all over with black lightning on my limbs. I wore a black mask, and across my forehead a single eagle feather hung.

When the horses and the men were painted they looked beautiful; but they looked fearful too.

The men were naked, except for a breech-clout; but the four maidens wore buckskin dresses dyed scarlet, and their faces were scarlet too. Their hair was braided, and they had wreaths of the sweet and cleansing sage, the sacred sage, around their heads, and from the wreath of each in front a single eagle feather hung. They were very beautiful to see.

All this time I was in the sacred tepee with the Six Grandfathers, and the four sacred virgins were in there too. No one outside was to see me until the dance began.

Right in the middle of the tepee the Grandfathers made a circle in the ground with a little trench, and across this they painted two roads—the red one running north and south, the black one, east and west. On the west side of this they placed a cup of water with a little bow and arrow laid across it; and on the east they painted the daybreak star. Then to the maiden who would represent the north they gave the healing herb to carry and a white goose wing, the cleansing wind. To her of the east they gave the holy pipe. To her of the south they gave the flowering stick; and to her who would represent the west they gave the nation's hoop. Thus the four maidens, good and beautiful, held in their hands the life of the nation.

All I carried was a red stick to represent the sacred arrow, the power of the thunder beings of the west.

We were now ready to begin the dance. The Six Grandfathers began to sing, announcing the riders of the different quarters. First they sang of the black horse riders, like this:

"They will appear—may you behold them!
 They will appear—may you behold them!
 A horse nation will appear.
 A thunder-being nation will appear.
 They will appear, behold!
 They will appear, behold!"

139

Then the black riders mounted their horses and stood four abreast facing the place where the sun goes down.

Next the Six Grandfathers sang:

"They will appear, may you behold them!
A horse nation will appear, behold!
A geese nation will appear, may you behold!"

Then the four white horsemen mounted and stood four abreast, facing the place where the White Giant lives.

Next the Six Grandfathers sang:

"Where the sun shines continually, they will
appear!
A buffalo nation, they will appear, behold!
A horse nation, they will appear, may you be-
hold!"

Then the red horsemen mounted and stood four abreast facing the east.

Next the Grandfathers sang:

"Where you are always facing, an elk nation
will appear!
May you behold!
A horse nation will appear,
Behold!"

The four yellow riders mounted their buckskins and stood four abreast facing the south.

Now it was time for me to go forth from the sacred tepee, but before I went forth I sang this song to the drums of the Grandfathers:

"He will appear, may you behold him!
An eagle for the eagle nation will appear.
May you behold!"

While I was singing thus in the sacred tepee I
could hear my horse snorting and prancing outside.
The virgins went forth four abreast and I followed
them, mounting my horse and standing behind them
facing the west.

Next the Six Grandfathers came forth and stood
abreast behind my bay, and they began to sing a
rapid, lively song to the drums, like this:

"They are dancing.
They are coming to behold you.
The horse nation of the west is dancing.
They are coming to behold!"

Then they sang the same of the horses of the
north and of the east and of the south. And as they
sang of each troop in turn, it wheeled and came and
took its place behind the Grandfathers—the blacks,
the whites, the sorrels and the buckskins, standing
four abreast and facing the west. They came pranc-
ing to the lively air of the Grandfathers' song, and
they pranced as they stood in line. And all the while
my bay was rearing too and prancing to the music
of the sacred song.

Now when we were all in line, facing the west,
I looked up into a dark cloud that was coming there
and the people all became quiet and the horses
quit prancing. And when there was silence but for
low thunder yonder, I sent a voice to the spirits of
the cloud, holding forth my right hand, thus, palm
outward, as I cried four times:

"Hey-a-a-hey! hey-a-a-hey! hey-a-a-hey! hey-a-a-hey!"

Then the Grandfathers behind me sang another sacred song from my vision, the one that goes like this:

"At the center of the earth, behold a four-
 legged.
 They have said this to me!"

And as they sang, a strange thing happened. My bay pricked up his ears and raised his tail and pawed the earth, neighing long and loud to where the sun goes down. And the four black horses raised their voices, neighing long and loud, and the whites and the sorrels and the buckskins did the same; and all the other horses in the village neighed, and even those out grazing in the valley and on the hill slopes raised their heads and neighed together. Then suddenly, as I sat there looking at the cloud, I saw my vision yonder once again—the tepee built of cloud and sewed with lightning, the flaming rainbow door and, underneath, the Six Grandfathers sitting, and all the horses thronging in their quarters; and also there was I myself upon my bay before the tepee. I looked about me and could see that what we then were doing was like a shadow cast upon the earth from yonder vision in the heavens, so bright it was and clear. I knew the real was yonder and the darkened dream of it was here.

And as I looked, the Six Grandfathers yonder in the cloud and all the riders of the horses, and even I myself upon the bay up there, all held their hands palms outward toward me, and when they did this, I had to pray, and so I cried:

"Grandfathers, you behold me!
 Spirits of the World, you behold!
 What you have said to me, I am now perform-
 ing!
 Hear me and help me!"

Then the vision went out, and the thunder cloud was coming on with lightning on its front and many voices in it, and the split-tail swallows swooped above us in a swarm.

The people of the village ran to fasten down their tepees, while the black horse riders sang to the drums that rolled like thunder, and this is what they sang:

"I myself made them fear.
 Myself, I wore an eagle relic.
 I myself made them fear.
 Myself, a lightning power I wore.
 I myself made them fear,
 Made them fear.
 The power of the hail I wore,
 I myself made them fear,
 Made them fear!
 Behold me!"

And as they sang, the hail and rain were falling yonder just a little way from us, and we could see it, but the cloud stood there and flashed and thundered, and only a little sprinkle fell on us. The thunder beings were glad and had come in a great crowd to see the dance.

Now the four virgins held high the sacred relics that they carried, the herb and the white wing, the

sacred pipe, the flowering stick, the nation's hoop, offering these to the spirits of the west. Then people who were sick or sad came to the virgins, making scarlet offerings to them, and after they had done this, they all felt better and some were cured of sickness and began to dance for joy.

Now the Grandfathers beat their drums again and the dance began. The four black horsemen, who had stood behind the Grandfathers, went ahead of the virgins, riding toward the west side of the circled village, and all the others followed in their order while the horses pranced and reared.

When the black horse troop had reached the western side, it wheeled around and fell to the rear behind the buckskins, and the white horse band came up and led until it reached the north side of the village. Then these fell back and took the rear behind the blacks, and the sorrels led until they reached the east. Then these fell back behind the whites, and the buckskins led until they reached the south. Then they fell back and took the rear, so that the blacks were leading as before toward the western quarter that was theirs. Each time the leading horse troop reached its quarter, the Six Grandfathers sang of the powers of that quarter, and there my bay faced, pricking up his ears and neighing loud, till all the other horses raised their voices neighing. When I thus faced the north, I sent a voice again and said: "Grandfather, behold me! What you gave me I have given to the people—the power of the healing herb and the cleansing wind. Thus my nation is made over. Hear and help me!"

And when we reached the east, and after the Grandfathers had sung, I sent a voice: "Grandfather, behold me! My people, with difficulty they walk.

Give them wisdom and guide them. Hear and help me!"

Between each quarter, as we marched and danced, we all sang together:

> "A horse nation all over the universe,
> Neighing, they come!
> Prancing, they come!
> May you behold them."

When we had reached the south and the Grandfathers had sung of the power of growing, my horse faced yonder and neighed again, and all the horses raised their voices as before. And then I prayed with hand upraised: "Grandfather, the flowering stick you gave me and the nation's sacred hoop I have given to the people. Hear me, you who have the power to make grow! Guide the people that they may be as blossoms on your holy tree, and make it flourish deep in Mother Earth and make it full of leaves and singing birds."

Then once more the blacks were leading, and as we marched and sang and danced toward the quarter of the west, the black hail cloud, still standing yonder watching, filled with voices crying: "Hey-hey! hey-hey!" They were cheering and rejoicing that my work was being done. And all the people now were happy and rejoicing, sending voices back, "hey-hey, hey-hey"; and all the horses neighed, rejoicing with the spirits and the people. Four times we marched and danced around the circle of the village, singing as we went, the leaders changing at the quarters, the Six Grandfathers singing to the power of each quarter, and to each I sent a voice. And at each quarter, as we stood, somebody who was sick or sad would

145

come with offerings to the virgins—little scarlet bags of the chacun sha sha, the red willow bark. And when the offering was made, the giver would feel better and begin to dance with joy.

And on the second time around, many of the people who had horses joined the dance with them, milling round and round the Six Grandfathers and the virgins as we danced ahead. And more and more got on their horses, milling round us as we went, until there was a whirl of prancing horses all about us at the end, and all the others danced afoot behind us, and everybody sang what we were singing.

When we reached the quarter of the west the fourth time, we stopped in new formation, facing inward toward the sacred tepee in the center of the village. First stood the virgins, next I stood upon the bay; then came the Six Grandfathers with eight riders on either side of them—the sorrels and the buckskins on their right hand, the blacks and whites upon their left. And when we stood so, the oldest of the Grandfathers, he who was the Spirit of the Sky, cried out: "Let all the people be ready. He shall send a voice four times, and at the last voice you shall go forth and coup the sacred tepee, and who shall coup it first shall have new power!"

All the riders were eager for the charge, and even the horses seemed to understand and were rearing and trying to get away. Then I raised my hand and cried hey-hey four times, and at the fourth the riders all yelled "hoka hey," and charged upon the tepee. My horse plunged inward along with all the others, but many were ahead of me and many couped the tepee before I did.

Then the horses were all rubbed down with sacred

sage and led away, and we began going into the
tepee to see what might have happened there while
we were dancing. The Grandfathers had sprinkled
fresh soil on the nation's hoop that they had made
in there with the red and black roads across it, and
all around this little circle of the nation's hoop we
saw the prints of tiny pony hoofs as though the
spirit horses had been dancing while we danced.

Now Black Road, who had helped me to perform
the dance, took the sacred pipe from the virgin of
the east. After filling it with chacun sha sha, the
bark of the red willow, he lit and offered it to the
Powers of the World, sending a voice thus:

"Grandfathers, you where the sun goes down, you
of the sacred wind where the white giant lives, you
where the day comes forth and the morning star,
you where lives the power to grow, you of the sky
and you of the earth, wings of the air and four-
leggeds of the world, behold! I, myself, with my
horse nation have done what I was to do on earth.
To all of you I offer this pipe that my people may
live!"

Then he smoked and passed the pipe. It went
all over the village until every one had smoked at
least a puff.

After the horse dance was over, it seemed that
I was above the ground and did not touch it when
I walked. I felt very happy, for I could see that my
people were all happier. Many crowded around me
and said that they or their relatives who had been
feeling sick were well again, and these gave me many
gifts. Even the horses seemed to be healthier and
happier after the dance.

The fear that was on me so long was gone, and
when thunder clouds appeared I was always glad

147

to see them, for they came as relatives now to visit me. Everything seemed good and beautiful now, and kind.

Before this, the medicine men would not talk to me, but now they would come to me to talk about my vision.

From that time on, I always got up very early to see the rising of the daybreak star. People knew that I did this, and many would get up to see it with me, and when it came we said: "Behold the star of understanding!"

XV

The Dog Vision

We stayed there near the mouth of the Tongue until
the end of the Moon of Making Fat (June). Then
the soldier chief told us that we could not be in
that country because we had sold it and it was not
ours any more. We had not sold it; but the soldiers
took all the rest of our horses from us and what guns
we had and loaded us on a big fire-boat that carried
us down the Yellowstone and the Missouri to Fort
Yates. There they unloaded us, and it was one of
the new reservations they had made for the Lakota.
Many of Sitting Bull's and Gall's people were there,
but Gall and Sitting Bull were still in Grandmoth-
er's Land. The soldiers had taken the ponies away
from all our people, and they said the Great Father
in Washington would pay us for them; but if he ever
did I have not heard of it.

I learned that my own band, the Ogalalas, had
been taken back to the country where we are now,
and I decided that I ought to go there and perform
my duty. So in the Moon When the Plums Are
Scarlet (September) I started with three others. We
had to go afoot and we had only bows and arrows
for weapons.

The Brules had been taken to the place where they are now on Rosebud Creek while I was in Grandmother's Land, and we set out first for where they were, camping seven times on the way.

One evening we crossed Smoky Earth River (the White) and camped on the south side. We camped by a plum thicket, and the plums were ripe. That is all we had to eat. There was a bluff close by, and I went up there alone and sat down with my face to where the sun was setting. It was a clear evening with no wind, and it seemed that everything was listening hard to hear something. While I was looking over there I felt that somebody wanted to talk to me. So I stood up and began to sing the first song of my vision, the one that the two spirits had sung to me.

"Behold! A sacred voice is calling you!
All over the sky a sacred voice is calling!"

While I was singing this song, suddenly the two men of my vision were coming again out of the sunset, head first like arrows slanting down. They were pointing at me with their bows. Then they stopped and stood, raising their bows above their heads and looking at me. They said nothing, but I could feel what they wanted. It was that I should do my duty among the Ogalalas with the power they had brought me in the vision. I stood there singing to them, and afterwhile they turned around and went back into the sunset, head first like arrows flying.

When I went back to our little camp by the plum thicket, the others there, who knew of my power and had heard me on the bluff, asked what I had

seen up there. I told them I was only singing to some people I knew in the outer world.

I stayed only a little while among the Brules on Rosebud Creek, and then I came on alone to White Clay Creek where the Wasichus were building Pine Ridge Agency for the Ogalalas. Our people called it the Seat of Red Cloud or the Place Where Everything Is Disputed. There I stayed, and that winter in the Moon of Popping Trees I was eighteen years old.[1]

That was a very hard winter, and it was just like one long night, with me lying awake, waiting and waiting and waiting for daybreak. For now the thunder beings were like relatives to me and they had gone away when the frost came and would not come back until the grasses showed their tender faces again. Without them I felt lost, and I was alone there among my people. Very few of them had seen the horse dance or knew anything about my vision and the power that it gave me. They seemed heavy, heavy and dark; and they could not know that they were heavy and dark. I could feel them like a great burden upon me; but when I would go all through my vision again, I loved the burden and felt pity for my people.

And now when I look about me upon my people in despair, I feel like crying and I wish and wish my vision could have been given to a man more worthy. I wonder why it came to me, a pitiful old man who can do nothing. Men and women and children I have cured of sickness with the power the vision gave me; but my nation I could not help. If a man or woman or child dies, it does not matter long, for the nation lives on. It was the nation that was dying, and the

[1] December, 1881.

vision was for the nation; but I have done nothing with it.

When I was still young, I could feel the power all through me, and it seemed that with the whole outer world to help me I could do anything.

I had made a good start to fulfill my duty to the Grandfathers, but I had much more to do; and so the winter was like a long night of waiting for the daybreak.

When the grasses began to show their faces again, I was happy, for I could hear the thunder beings coming in the earth and I could hear them saying: "It is time to do the work of your Grandfathers."

After the long winter of waiting, it was my first duty to go out lamenting. So after the first rain storm I began to get ready.

When going out to lament it is necessary to choose a wise old medicine man, who is quiet and generous, to help. He must fill and offer the pipe to the Six Powers and to the four-leggeds and the wings of the air, and he must go along to watch. There was a good and wise old medicine man by the name of Few Tails, who was glad to help me. First he told me to fast four days, and I could have only water during that time. Then, after he had offered the pipe, I had to purify myself in a sweat lodge, which we made with willow boughs set in the ground and bent down to make a round top. Over this we tied a bison robe. In the middle we put hot stones, and when I was in there, Few Tails poured water on the stones. I sang to the spirits while I was in there being purified. Then the old man rubbed me all over with the sacred sage. He then braided my hair, and I was naked except that I had a bison robe to wrap around me while lamenting in the night,

for although the days were warm, the nights were
cold yet. All I carried was the sacred pipe.

It is necessary to go far away from people to
lament, so Few Tails and I started from Pine Ridge
toward where we are now.[2]

We came to a high hill close to Grass Creek,
which is just a little way west from here. There was
nobody there but the old man and myself and the sky
and the earth. But the place was full of people; for
the spirits were there.

The sun was almost setting when we came to the
hill, and the old man helped me make the place
where I was to stand. We went to the highest point
of the hill and made the ground there sacred by
spreading sage upon it. Then Few Tails set a flower-
ing stick in the middle of the place, and on the west,
the north, the east, and the south sides of it he
placed offerings of red willow bark tied into little
bundles with scarlet cloth.

Few Tails now told me what I was to do so that
the spirits would hear me and make clear my next
duty. I was to stand in the middle, crying and
praying for understanding. Then I was to advance
from the center to the quarter of the west and mourn
there awhile. Then I was to back up to the center,
and from there approach the quarter of the north,
wailing and praying there, and so on all around the
circle. This I had to do all night long.

It was time for me to begin lamenting, so Few
Tails went away somewhere and left me there all
alone on the hill with the spirits and the dying light.

Standing in the center of the sacred place and
facing the sunset, I began to cry, and while crying

[2] Black Elk's home near Manderson P. O., South Dakota.

I had to say: "O Great Spirit, accept my offerings! O make me understand!"

As I was crying and saying this, there soared a spotted eagle from the west and whistled shrill and sat upon a pine tree east of me.

I walked backwards to the center, and from there approached the north, crying and saying: "O Great Spirit, accept my offerings and make me understand!" Then a chicken hawk came hovering and stopped upon a bush towards the south.

I walked backwards to the center once again and from there approached the east, crying and asking the Great Spirit to help me understand, and there came a black swallow flying all around me, singing, and stopped upon a bush not far away.

Walking backwards to the center, I advanced upon the south. Until now I had only been trying to weep, but now I really wept, and the tears ran down my face; for as I looked yonder towards the place whence come the life of things, the nation's hoop and the flowering tree, I thought of the days when my relatives, now dead, were living and young, and of Crazy Horse who was our strength and would never come back to help us any more.

I cried very hard, and I thought it might be better if my crying would kill me; then I could be in the outer world where nothing is ever in despair.

And while I was crying, something was coming from the south. It looked like dust far off, but when it came closer, I saw it was a cloud of beautiful butterflies of all colors. They swarmed around me so thick that I could see nothing else.

I walked backwards to the flowering stick again, and the spotted eagle on the pine tree spoke and

said: "Behold these! They are your people. They
are in great difficulty and you shall help them."
Then I could hear all the butterflies that were swarm-
ing over me, and they were all making a pitiful,
whimpering noise as though they too were weeping.

Then they all arose and flew back into the south.

Now the chicken hawk spoke from its bush and
said: "Behold! Your Grandfathers shall come forth
and you shall hear them!"

Hearing this, I lifted up my eyes, and there was
a big storm coming from the west. It was the thun-
der being nation, and I could hear the neighing of
horses and the sending of great voices.

It was very dark now, and all the roaring west
was streaked fearfully with swift fire.

And as I stood there looking, a vision broke out
of the shouting blackness torn with fire, and I saw
the two men who had come to me first in my great
vision. They came head first like arrows slanting
earthward from a long flight; and when they neared
the ground, I could see a dust rising there and out of
the dust the heads of dogs were peeping. Then sud-
denly I saw that the dust was the swarm of many-
colored butterflies hovering all around and over the
dogs.

By now the two men were riding sorrel horses,
streaked with black lightning, and they charged with
bows and arrows down upon the dogs, while the
thunder beings cheered for them with roaring voices.

Then suddenly the butterflies changed, and were
storm-driven swallows, swooping and whirling in a
great cloud behind the charging riders.

The first of these now plunged upon a dog's head
and arose with it hanging bloody on his arrow point,

155

while the whole west roared with cheering. The second did the same; and the black west flashed and cheered again. Then as the two arose together, I saw that the dogs' heads had changed to the heads of Wasichus; and as I saw, the vision went out and the storm was close upon me, terrible to see and roaring.

I cried harder than ever now, for I was much afraid. The night was black about me and terrible with swift fire and the sending of great voices and the roaring of the hail. And as I cried, I begged the Grandfathers to pity me and spare me and told them that I knew now what they wanted me to do on earth, and I would do it if I could.

All at once I was not afraid any more, and I thought that if I was killed, probably I might be better off in the other world. So I lay down there in the center of the sacred place and offered the pipe again. Then I drew the bison robe over me and waited. All around me growled and roared the voices, and the hail was like the drums of many giants beating while the giants sang: "Hey-a-hey!"

No hail fell there in the sacred circle where I lay, nor any rain. And when the storm was passed, I raised my robe and listened; and in the stillness I could hear the rain-flood singing in the gulches all around me in the darkness, and far away to eastward there were dying voices calling: "Hey-a-hey!"

The night was old by now, and soon I fell asleep. And as I slept I saw my people sitting sad and troubled all around a sacred tepee, and there were many who were sick. And as I looked on them and wept, a strange light leaped upward from the ground close by—a light of many colors, sparkling, with rays

that touched the heavens. Then it was gone, and in the place from whence it sprang a herb was growing and I saw the leaves it had. And as I was looking at the herb so that I might not forget it, there was a voice that 'woke me, and it said: "Make haste! Your people need you!"

I looked and saw the east was just beginning to turn white. Standing up, I faced the young light and began to mourn again and pray. Then the daybreak star came slowly, very beautiful and still; and all around it there were clouds of baby faces smiling at me, the faces of the people not yet born. The stars about them now were beautiful with many colors, and beneath these there were heads of men and women moving around, and birds were singing somewhere yonder and there were horses nickering and blowing as they do when they are happy, and somewhere deer were whistling and there were bison mooing too. What I could not see of this, I heard.

I think I fell asleep again, for afterwhile I was startled by a voice that said: "Get up, I have come after you!" I looked to see a spirit, but it was the good old man, Few Tails, standing over me. And now the sun was rising.

So we brought the sacred pipe back home and I went into the sweat lodge after offering the pipe to the Six Powers. When I was purified again, some very old men who were good and wise asked me to tell them what I had heard and seen. So after offering and smoking the sacred pipe again, I told it all to them, and they said that I must perform the dog vision on earth to help the people, and because the people were discouraged and sad, I should do this with heyokas, who are sacred fools, doing everything wrong or backwards to make the people laugh.

They said they did not know but I would be a great man, because not many men were called to see such visions. I must wait twenty days, they said, and then perform my duty. So I waited.

XVI

Heyoka Ceremony

Twenty days passed, and it was time to perform the dog vision with heyokas. But before I tell you how we did it, I will say something about heyokas and the heyoka ceremony, which seems to be very foolish, but is not so.

Only those who have had visions of the thunder beings of the west can act as heyokas. They have sacred power and they share some of this with all the people, but they do it through funny actions. When a vision comes from the thunder beings of the west, it comes with terror like a thunder storm; but when the storm of vision has passed, the world is greener and happier; for wherever the truth of vision comes upon the world, it is like a rain. The world, you see, is happier after the terror of the storm.

But in the heyoka ceremony, everything is backwards, and it is planned that the people shall be made to feel jolly and happy first, so that it may be easier for the power to come to them. You have noticed that the truth comes into this world with two faces. One is sad with suffering, and the other laughs; but it is the same face, laughing or weeping. When people are already in despair, maybe the

laughing is better for them; and when they feel too
good and are too sure of being safe, maybe the
weeping face is better for them to see. And so I
think that is what the heyoka ceremony is for.

There was a man by the name of Wachpanne
(Poor) who took charge of this ceremony for me,
because he had acted as a heyoka many times and
knew all about it. First he told all the people to
gather in a circle on the flat near Pine Ridge, and
in the center, near a sacred tepee that was set there,
he placed a pot of water which was made to boil
by dropping hot stones from a fire into it. First, he
had to make an offering of sweet grass to the west.
He sat beside the fire with some sweet grass in his
hand, and said: "To the Great Spirit's day, to that
day grown old and wise, I will make an offering."
Then, as he sprinkled the grass upon the fire and the
sweet smoke arose, he sang:

> "This I burn as an offering.
> Behold it!
> A sacred praise I am making.
> A sacred praise I am making.
> My nation, behold it in kindness!
> The day of the sun has been my strength.
> The path of the moon shall be my robe.
> A sacred praise I am making.
> A sacred praise I am making."

Then the dog had to be killed quickly and with-
out making any scar, as lightning kills, for it is the
power of the lightning that heyokas have.

Over the smoke of the sweet grass a rawhide rope
was held to make it sacred. Then two heyokas tied
a slip noose in the rope and put this over the neck

of the dog. Three times they pulled the rope gently, one at each end of the rope, and the fourth time they jerked it hard, breaking the neck. Then Wachpanne singed the dog and washed it well, and after that he cut away everything but the head, the spine and the tail. Now walking six steps away from the pot, one for each of the Powers, he turned to the west, offering the head and spine to the thunder beings, then to the north, the east and the south, then to the Spirit above and to Mother Earth.

After this, standing where he was, six steps away, he faced the pot and said: "In a sacred manner I thus boil this dog." Three times he swung it, and the fourth time he threw it so that it fell head first into the boiling water. Then he took the heart of the dog and did with it just what he had done with the head and spine.

During all this time, thirty heyokas, one for each day of a moon, were doing foolish tricks among the people to make them feel jolly. They were all dressed and painted in such funny ways that everybody who saw them had to laugh. One Side and I were fellow clowns. We had our bodies painted red all over and streaked with black lightning. The right sides of our heads were shaved, and the hair on the left side was left hanging long. This looked very funny, but it had a meaning; for when we looked toward where you are always facing (the south) the bare sides of our heads were toward the west, which showed that we were humble before the thunder beings who had given us power. Each of us carried a very long bow, so long that nobody could use it, and it was very crooked too. The arrows that we carried were very long and very crooked, so that it looked crazy to have them. We were riding sorrels

with streaks of black lightning all over them, for we were to represent the two men of my dog vision.

Wachpanne now went into the sacred tepee, where he sang about the heyokas:

> "These are sacred,
> These are sacred,
> They have said,
> They have said.
> These are sacred,
> They have said."

Twelve times he sang this, once for each of the moons.

Afterward, while the pot was boiling, One Side and I, sitting on our painted sorrels, faced the west and sang:

> "In a sacred manner they have sent voices.
> Half the universe has sent voices.
> In a sacred manner they have sent voices to
> you."

Even while we were singing thus, the heyokas were doing foolish things and making laughter. For instance, two heyokas with long crooked bows and arrows painted in a funny way would come to a little shallow puddle of water. They would act as though they thought it was a wide, deep river that they had to cross; so, making motions, but saying nothing, they would decide to see how deep the river was. Taking their long crooked arrows, they would thrust these into the water, not downwards, but flat-wise just under the surface. This would make

162

the whole arrow wet. Standing the arrows up beside them, they would show that the water was far over their heads in depth, so they would get ready to swim. One would then plunge into the shallow puddle head first, getting his face in the mud and fighting the water wildly as though he were drowning. Then the other one would plunge in to save his comrade, and there would be more funny antics in the water to make the people laugh.

After One Side and I had sung to the west, we faced the pot, where the heart and the head of the dog had been boiling. With sharp pointed arrows, we charged on horseback upon the pot and past it. I had to catch the head upon my arrow and One Side had to catch the heart, for we were representing the two men I had seen in the vision. After we had done this, the heyokas all chased us, trying to get a piece of the meat, and the people rushed to the pot, trying to get a piece of the sacred flesh. Ever so little of it would be good for them, for the power of the west was in it now. It was like giving them medicine to make them happier and stronger.

When the ceremony was over, everybody felt a great deal better, for it had been a day of fun. They were better able now to see the greenness of the world, the wideness of the sacred day, the colors of the earth, and to set these in their minds.

The Six Grandfathers have placed in their world many things, all of which should be happy. Every little thing is sent for something, and in that thing there should be happiness and the power to make happy. Like the grasses showing tender faces to each other, thus we should do, for this was the wish of the Grandfathers of the World.

XVII

The First Cure

After the heyoka ceremony, I came to live here where I am now between Wounded Knee Creek and Grass Creek. Others came too, and we made these little gray houses of logs that you see, and they are square. It is a bad way to live, for there can be no power in a square.

You have noticed that everything an Indian does is in a circle, and that is because the Power of the World always works in circles, and everything tries to be round. In the old days when we were a strong and happy people, all our power came to us from the sacred hoop of the nation, and so long as the hoop was unbroken, the people flourished. The flowering tree was the living center of the hoop, and the circle of the four quarters nourished it. The east gave peace and light, the south gave warmth, the west gave rain, and the north with its cold and mighty wind gave strength and endurance. This knowledge came to us from the outer world with our religion. Everything the Power of the World does is done in a circle. The sky is round, and I have heard that the earth is round like a ball, and so are all the stars. The wind, in its greatest power, whirls. Birds make their nests

in circles, for theirs is the same religion as ours. The sun comes forth and goes down again in a circle. The moon does the same, and both are round. Even

AN INDIAN WAY OF WRITING A NAME. IT INDICATES BLACK ELK.

the seasons form a great circle in their changing, and always come back again to where they were. The life of a man is a circle from childhood to childhood, and so it is in everything where power moves. Our tepees were round like the nests of birds, and these were always set in a circle, the nation's hoop, a nest of many nests, where the Great Spirit meant for us to hatch our children.

But the Wasichus have put us in these square boxes. Our power is gone and we are dying, for the power is not in us any more. You can look at our boys and see how it is with us. When we were living by the power of the circle in the way we should, boys were men at twelve or thirteen years of age. But now it takes them very much longer to mature.

Well, it is as it is. We are prisoners of war while we are waiting here. But there is another world.

It was in the Moon of Shedding Ponies (May) when we had the heyoka ceremony. One day in the Moon of Fatness (June), when everything was blooming, I invited One Side to come over and eat with me. I had been thinking about the four-rayed herb that I had now seen twice—the first time in the great vision when I was nine years old, and the second time when I was lamenting on the hill. I knew that I must have this herb for curing, and I thought I could recognize the place where I had seen it growing that night when I lamented.

After One Side and I had eaten, I told him there was a herb I must find, and I wanted him to help me hunt for it. Of course I did not tell him I had seen it in a vision. He was willing to help, so we got on our horses and rode over to Grass Creek. Nobody was living over there. We came to the top of a high hill above the creek, and there we got off our horses and sat down, for I felt that we were close to where I saw the herb growing in my vision of the dog.

We sat there awhile singing together some heyoka songs. Then I began to sing alone a song I had heard in my first great vision:

"In a sacred manner they are sending voices."

After I had sung this song, I looked down towards the west, and yonder at a certain spot beside the creek were crows and magpies, chicken hawks and spotted eagles circling around and around.

Then I knew, and I said to One Side: "Friend, right there is where the herb is growing." He said: "We will go forth and see." So we got on our horses and rode down Grass Creek until we came to a dry gulch, and this we followed up. As we neared the spot the birds all flew away, and it was a place where four or five dry gulches came together. There right on the side of the bank the herb was growing, and I knew it, although I had never seen one like it before, except in my vision.

It had a root about as long as to my elbow, and this was a little thicker than my thumb. It was flowering in four colors, blue, white, red, and yellow.

We got off our horses, and after I had offered red willow bark to the Six Powers, I made a prayer to the herb, and said to it: "Now we shall go forth to the two-leggeds, but only to the weakest ones, and there shall be happy days among the weak."

It was easy to dig the herb, because it was growing in the edge of the clay gulch. Then we started back with it. When we came to Grass Creek again, we wrapped it in some good sage that was growing there.

Something must have told me to find the herb just then, for the next evening I needed it and could have done nothing without it.

I was eating supper when a man by the name of Cuts-to-Pieces came in, and he was saying: "Hey, hey, hey!" for he was in trouble. I asked him what was the matter, and he said: "I have a boy of mine, and he is very sick and I am afraid he will die

soon. He has been sick a long time. They say you have great power from the horse dance and the heyoka ceremony, so maybe you can save him for me. I think so much of him."

I told Cuts-to-Pieces that if he really wanted help, he should go home and bring me back a pipe with an eagle feather on it. While he was gone, I thought about what I had to do; and I was afraid, because I had never cured anybody yet with my power, and I was very sorry for Cuts-to-Pieces. I prayed hard for help. When Cuts-to-Pieces came back with the pipe, I told him to take it around to the left of me, leave it there, and pass out again to the right of me. When he had done this, I sent for One Side to come and help me. Then I took the pipe and went to where the sick little boy was. My father and my mother went with us, and my friend, Standing Bear, was already there.

I first offered the pipe to the Six Powers, then I passed it, and we all smoked. After that I began making a rumbling thunder sound on the drum. You know, when the power of the west comes to the two-leggeds, it comes with rumbling, and when it has passed, everything lifts up its head and is glad and there is greenness. So I made this rumbling sound. Also, the voice of the drum is an offering to the Spirit of the World. Its sound arouses the mind and makes men feel the mystery and power of things.

The sick little boy was on the northeast side of the tepee, and when we entered at the south, we went around from left to right, stopping on the west side when we had made the circle.

You want to know why we always go from left to right like that. I can tell you something of the reason, but not all. Think of this: Is not the south

the source of life, and does not the flowering stick truly come from there? And does not man advance from there toward the setting sun of his life? Then does he not approach the colder north where the white hairs are? And does he not then arrive, if he lives, at the source of light and understanding, which is the east? Then does he not return to where he began, to his second childhood, there to give back his life to all life, and his flesh to the earth whence it came? The more you think about this, the more meaning you will see in it.

As I said, we went into the tepee from left to right, and sat ourselves down on the west side. The sick little boy was on the northeast side, and he looked as though he were only skin and bones. I had the pipe, the drum and the four-rayed herb already, so I asked for a wooden cup, full of water, and an eagle bone whistle, which was for the spotted eagle of my great vision. They placed the cup of water in front of me; and then I had to think awhile, because I had never done this before and I was in doubt.

I understood a little more now, so I gave the eagle bone whistle to One Side and told him how to use it in helping me. Then I filled the pipe with red willow bark, and gave it to the pretty young daughter of Cuts-to-Pieces, telling her to hold it, just as I had seen the virgin of the east holding it in my great vision.

Everything was ready now, so I made low thunder on the drum, keeping time as I sent forth a voice. Four times I cried "Hey-a-a-hey," drumming as I cried to the Spirit of the World, and while I was doing this I could feel the power coming through

me from my feet up, and I knew that I could help the sick little boy.

I kept on sending a voice, while I made low thunder on the drum, saying: "My Grandfather, Great Spirit, you are the only one and to no other can any one send voices. You have made everything, they say, and you have made it good and beautiful. The four quarters and the two roads crossing each other, you have made. Also you have set a power where the sun goes down. The two-leggeds on earth are in despair. For them, my Grandfather, I send a voice to you. You have said this to me: The weak shall walk. In vision you have taken me to the center of the world and there you have shown me the power to make over. The water in the cup that you have given me, by its power shall the dying live. The herb that you have shown me, through its power shall the feeble walk upright. From where we are always facing (the south), behold, a virgin shall appear, walking the good red road, offering the pipe as she walks, and hers also is the power of the flowering tree. From where the Giant lives (the north), you have given me a sacred, cleansing wind, and where this wind passes the weak shall have strength. You have said this to me. To you and to all your powers and to Mother Earth I send a voice for help."

You see, I had never done this before, and I know now that only one power would have been enough. But I was so eager to help the sick little boy that I called on every power there is.

I had been facing the west, of course, while sending a voice. Now I walked to the north and to the east and to the south, stopping there where the source of all life is and where the good red road begins. Standing there, I sang thus:

"In a sacred manner I have made them walk.
A sacred nation lies low.
In a sacred manner I have made them walk.
A sacred two-legged, he lies low.
In a sacred manner, he shall walk."

While I was singing this I could feel something queer all through my body, something that made me want to cry for all unhappy things, and there were tears on my face.

Now I walked to the quarter of the west, where I lit the pipe, offered it to the powers, and, after I had taken a whiff of smoke, I passed it around.

When I looked at the sick little boy again, he smiled at me, and I could feel that the power was getting stronger.

I next took the cup of water, drank a little of it, and went around to where the sick little boy was. Standing before him, I stamped the earth four times. Then, putting my mouth to the pit of his stomach, I drew through him the cleansing wind of the north. I next chewed some of the herb and put it in the water, afterward blowing some of it on the boy and to the four quarters. The cup with the rest of the water I gave to the virgin, who gave it to the sick little boy to drink. Then I told the virgin to help the boy stand up and to walk around the circle with him, beginning at the south, the source of life. He was very poor and weak, but with the virgin's help he did this.

Then I went away.

Next day Cuts-to-Pieces came and told me that his little boy was feeling better and was sitting up and could eat something again. In four days he could walk around. He got well and lived to be thirty years old.

Cuts-to-Pieces gave me a good horse for doing this; but of course I would have done it for nothing.

When the people heard about how the little boy was cured, many came to me for help, and I was busy most of the time.

This was in the summer of my nineteenth year (1882), in the Moon of Making Fat.

XVIII

The Powers of the Bison
and the Elk

I think I have told you, but if I have not, you must
have understood, that a man who has a vision is
not able to use the power of it until after he has
performed the vision on earth for the people to see.
You remember that my great vision came to me
when I was only nine years old, and you have
seen that I was not much good for anything until
after I had performed the horse dance near the
mouth of the Tongue River during my eighteenth
summer. And if the great fear had not come upon
me, as it did, and forced me to do my duty, I might
have been less good to the people than some man
who had never dreamed at all, even with the mem-
ory of so great a vision in me. But the fear came,
and if I had not obeyed it, I am sure it would have
killed me in a little while.

It was even then only after the heyoka ceremony,
in which I performed my dog vision, that I had the
power to practice as a medicine man, curing sick
people; and many I cured with the power that came
through me. Of course it was not I who cured. It

was the power from the outer world, and the visions and ceremonies had only made me like a hole through which the power could come to the two-leggeds. If I thought that I was doing it myself, the hole would close up and no power could come through. Then everything I could do would be foolish. There were other parts of my great vision that I still had to perform before I could use the power that was in those parts. If you think about my great vision again, you will remember how the red man turned into a bison and rolled, and that the people found the good red road after that. If you will read again what is written, you will see how it was.

To use the power of the bison, I had to perform that part of my vision for the people to see. It was during the summer of my first cure that this was done. I carried the pipe to Fox Belly, a wise and good old medicine man, and asked him to help me do this duty. He was glad to help me, but first I had to tell him how it was in that part of my vision. I did not tell him all my vision, only that part. I had never told any one all of it, and even until now nobody ever heard it all. Even my old friend, Standing Bear, and my son here have heard it now for the first time when I have told it to you. Of course there was very much in the vision that even I can not tell when I try hard, because very much of it was not for words. But I have told what can be told.

It has made me very sad to do this at last, and I have lain awake at night worrying and wondering if I was doing right; for I know I have given away my power when I have given away my vision, and maybe I cannot live very long now. But I think I have done right to save the vision in this way, even though I may die sooner because I did it; for

I know the meaning of the vision is wise and beautiful and good; and you can see that I am only a pitiful old man after all.

Well, I told Fox Belly all that he needed to know that he might help me. And when he had heard even so little, he said: "My boy, you had a great vision, and I can see that it is your duty to help the people walk the red road in a manner pleasing to the Powers."

This ceremony was not a long one, but it had great meaning, because it made a picture of the relation between the people and the bison, and the power was in the meaning.

First we made a sacred place like a bison wallow at the center of the nation's hoop, and there we set up the sacred tepee. Inside this we made the circle of the four quarters. Across the circle from south to north we painted a red road, and Fox Belly made little bison tracks all along on both sides of it, meaning that the people should walk there with the power and endurance of the bison, facing the great white cleansing wind of the world. Also, he placed at the north end of the road the cup of water, which is the gift of the west, so that the people, while leaning against the great wind with the endurance of bison, would be going toward the water of life.

I was painted red all over like the man of my vision before he turned into a bison. I wore bison horns, and on the left horn hung a piece of the day-break-star herb, which bears the four-rayed flower of understanding. On the left side of my body I wore a single eagle feather, which was for my people, hanging on the side of the bison and feeding there.

One Side had come over to help me in this ceremony too. He was painted red all over, and he car-

ried the drum and the pipe, and wherever I went, he followed, as the people follow the bison.

We stood inside the tepee at the south end of the good red road, and Fox Belly sang like this:

"Revealing this, they walk.
 A sacred herb—revealing it, they walk.
 Revealing this, they walk.
 The sacred life of bison—revealing it, they
 walk.
 Revealing this, they walk.
 A sacred eagle feather—revealing it, they
 walk.
 Revealing them, they walk.
 The eagle and the bison—like relatives they
 walk."

Then, after we had walked the red road, One Side and I went out of the tepee and the people flocked around us, and the sick came with scarlet offerings to be cured. We went all around among the people, acting like bison and making the sounds they make. Then we returned to the tepee, and there the people brought their little children to us, and to each I gave a little of the water of life from the wooden cup, that their feet might know the good red road that leads to health and happiness.

It is from understanding that power comes; and the power in the ceremony was in understanding what it meant; for nothing can live well except in a manner that is suited to the way the sacred Power of the World lives and moves.

After this, I went on curing sick people, and I was busy doing this. I was in doubt no longer. I

felt like a man, and I could feel the power with me all the time.

It was during the next summer, when I was in my twentieth year (1883), that I performed the elk ceremony, as a duty to that part of my great vision. You will remember how the pipe and the bison were in the east and the elk in the south.

This ceremony of the elk was to represent the source of life and the mystery of growing.

I sent a pipe to Running Elk, who was Standing Bear's uncle and a good and wise old man. He came and was willing to help me. We set up a sacred te-pee at the center as before. I had to use six elks and four virgins. The elks are of the south, but the power that they represented in my vision is nourished by the four quarters and from the sky and the earth; so there were six of them. The four virgins repre-sented the life of the nation's hoop, which has four quarters; so there were four virgins. Running Elk chose two of the elks, and I, who stood between the Power of the World and the nation's hoop, chose the four others, for my duty was to the life of the hoop on earth. The six elk men wore complete elk hides on their backs and over their heads. Their limbs were painted black from the knee and elbow down, and yellow from there up; for the growing power is rooted in mystery like the night, and reaches lightward. Seeds sprout in the darkness of the ground before they know the summer and the day. In the night of the womb the spirit quickens into flesh. The four virgins wore scarlet dresses, and each had a single eagle feather in her braided hair; for out of the woman the people grows, and the eagle feather again was for the people as in the bison ceremony. The faces of the virgins were painted yellow, the

177

color of the south, the source of life. One had a daybreak star in red upon her forehead. One had a crescent moon in blue, for the power of woman grows with the moon and comes and goes with it. One had the sun upon her forehead; and around the mouth and eyebrows of the fourth a big blue circle was painted to mean the nation's hoop. On the back of each of the elk men was painted the nation's hoop, for upon the backs of men the nation is carried, and in the center of each hoop hung a single eagle feather for the people. They had yellow masks upon their faces, for behind the woman's power of life is hidden the power of man. They all carried flowering sticks cut from the sacred rustling tree (the cottonwood) with leaves left at the top, and the sticks were painted red. The woman is the life of the flowering tree, but the man must feed and care for it. One of the virgins also carried the flowering stick, another carried the pipe which gives peace, a third bore the herb of healing and the fourth held the sacred hoop; for all these powers together are woman's power.

Of course, before any of this was done, those who were to take part were purified in the sweat lodge as always.

We were all inside the sacred tepee, and Running Elk sang this song:

> "Advancing to the quarters,
> Advancing to the quarters,
> They are coming to behold you.
> Advancing to the quarters,
> Advancing to the quarters,
> They are coming to behold you."

Then the elk men all made the elk sound, *unh, unh, unh*. Running Elk then sang again:

> "Singing, I send a voice as I walk.
> Singing, I send a voice as I walk.
> A sacred hoop I wear as I walk."

It was time now to come out of the sacred tepee: first came the virgin with the pipe; next she who bore the flowering stick, then the one who held the herb; and last, the bearer of the nation's hoop. The four virgins stood abreast, facing the west. Then we six elk men came out, snorting and stamping our feet. We stopped abreast, behind the virgins, who now held up the sacred things they carried, offering them to the thunder beings. When they had done this, they walked abreast to the north, while we elk men danced around them in a circle, and there they offered their sacred objects to the great white cleansing wind. In the same way we went to the east and to the south, the virgins making the offering at each place, and we elk men dancing around them in a circle all the while.

From the south, the four virgins turned straight north, following the good red road to the center of the village where the sacred tepee stood, and we elk men followed, dancing around them, for the power of the man encircles and protects the power of the woman.

The four maidens entered the tepee: first, she with the sacred hoop; then she who bore the flowering stick; next, the one who held the cleansing herb; and after her, the bearer of the pipe.

When they had all entered, we elk men followed into the tepee.

This was the ceremony, and as I said before, the power of it was in the understanding of its meaning; for nothing can live well except in a manner suited to the way the Power of the World lives and moves to do its work.

XIX

Across the Big Water

As I told you, it was in the summer of my twentieth
year (1883) that I performed the ceremony of the
elk. That fall, they say, the last of the bison herds
was slaughtered by the Wasichus. I can remember
when the bison were so many that they could not be
counted, but more and more Wasichus came to kill
them until there were only heaps of bones scattered
where they used to be. The Wasichus did not kill them
to eat; they killed them for the metal that makes
them crazy, and they took only the hides to sell.
Sometimes they did not even take the hides, only
the tongues; and I have heard that fire-boats came
down the Missouri River loaded with dried bison
tongues. You can see that the men who did this
were crazy. Sometimes they did not even take the
tongues; they just killed and killed because they liked
to do that. When we hunted bison, we killed only
what we needed. And when there was nothing left
but heaps of bones, the Wasichus came and gathered
up even the bones and sold them.

All our people now were settling down in square
gray houses, scattered here and there across this
hungry land, and around them the Wasichus had

drawn a line to keep them in. The nation's hoop was broken, and there was no center any longer for the flowering tree. The people were in despair. They seemed heavy to me, heavy and dark; so heavy that it seemed they could not be lifted; so dark that they could not be made to see any more. Hunger was among us often now, for much of what the Great Father in Washington sent us must have been stolen by Wasichus who were crazy to get money. There were many lies, but we could not eat them. The forked tongue made promises.

I kept on curing the sick for three years more, and many came to me and were made over; but when I thought of my great vision, which was to save the nation's hoop and make the holy tree to bloom in the center of it, I felt like crying, for the sacred hoop was broken and scattered. The life of the people was in the hoop, and what are many little lives if the life of those lives be gone?

But late in my twenty-third summer (1886), it seemed that there was a little hope. There came to us some Wasichus who wanted a band of Ogalalas for a big show that the other Pahuska[1] had. They told us this show would go across the big water to strange lands, and I thought I ought to go, because I might learn some secret of the Wasichu that would help my people somehow. In my great vision, when I stood at the center of the world, the two men from the east had brought me the daybreak-star herb and they had told me to drop it on the earth; and where it touched the ground it took root and bloomed four-rayed. It was the herb of understanding. Also, where the red man of my vision changed into a bison that

[1] Long Hair, Buffalo Bill.

rolled, the same herb grew and bloomed when the bison had vanished, and after that the people in my vision found the good red road again. Maybe if I could see the great world of the Wasichu, I could understand how to bring the sacred hoop together and make the tree to bloom again at the center of it.

I looked back on the past and recalled my people's old ways, but they were not living that way any more. They were traveling the black road, everybody for himself and with little rules of his own, as in my vision. I was in despair, and I even thought that if the Wasichus had a better way, then maybe my people should live that way. I know now that this was foolish, but I was young and in despair.

My relatives told me I should stay at home and go on curing people, but I would not listen to them.

The show people sent wagons from Rushville on the iron road to get us, and we were about a hundred men and women. Many of our people followed us half way to the iron road and there we camped and ate together. Afterward we left our people crying there, for we were going very far across the big water.

That evening where the big wagons were waiting for us on the iron road, we had a dance. Then we got into the wagons. When we started, it was dark, and thinking of my home and my people made me very sad. I wanted to get off and run back. But we went roaring all night long, and in the morning we ate at Long Pine. Then we started again and went roaring all day and came to a very big town in the evening.[2]

[2] Omaha.

Then we roared along all night again and came to a much bigger town.[3] There we stayed all day and all night; and right there I could compare my people's ways with Wasichu ways, and this made me sadder than before. I wished and wished that I had not gone away from home.

Then we went roaring on again, and afterwhile we came to a still bigger town—a very big town.[4] We walked through this town to the place where the show was.[5] Some Pawnees and Omahas were there, and when they saw us they made war-cries and charged, couping us. They were doing this for fun and because they felt glad to see us. I was surprised at the big houses and so many people, and there were bright lights at night, so that you could not see the stars, and some of these lights, I heard, were made with the power of thunder.

We stayed there and made shows for many, many Wasichus all that winter. I liked the part of the show we made, but not the part the Wasichus made. Afterwhile I got used to being there, but I was like a man who had never had a vision. I felt dead and my people seemed lost and I thought I might never find them again. I did not see anything to help my people. I could see that the Wasichus did not care for each other the way our people did before the nation's hoop was broken. They would take everything from each other if they could, and so there were some who had more of everything than they could use, while crowds of people had nothing at all and maybe were starving. They had forgotten that the earth was their mother. This could not be better

[3] Chicago.
[4] New York.
[5] Madison Square Garden.

than the old ways of my people. There was a pris-
oners' house on an island where the big water came
up to the town, and we saw that one day. Men
pointed guns at the prisoners and made them move
around like animals in a cage. This made me feel
very sad, because my people too were penned up in
islands, and maybe that was the way the Wasichus
were going to treat them.

In the spring it got warmer, but the Wasichus had
even the grass penned up. We heard then that we
were going to cross the big water to strange lands.
Some of our people went home and wanted me to go
with them, but I had not seen anything good for my
people yet; maybe across the big water there was
something to see, so I did not go home, although I
was sick and in despair.

They put us all on a very big fire-boat, so big
that when I first saw, I could hardly believe it; and
when it sent forth a voice, I was frightened. There
were other big fire-boats sending voices, and little
ones too.

Afterwhile I could see nothing but water, water,
water, and we did not seem to be going anywhere,
just up and down; but we were told that we were
going fast. If we were, I thought that we must drop
off where the water ended; or maybe we might have
to stop where the sky came down to the water. There
was nothing but mist where the big town used to be
and nothing but water all around.

We were all in despair now and many were feel-
ing so sick that they began to sing their death-songs.

When evening came, a big wind was roaring and
the water thundered. We had things that were meant
to be hung up while we slept in them. This I learned
afterward. We did not know what to do with these,

so we spread them out on the floor and lay down on them. The floor tipped in every direction, and this got worse and worse, so that we rolled from one side to the other and could not sleep. We were frightened, and now we were all very sick too. At first the Wasichus laughed at us; but very soon we could see that they were frightened too, because they were running around and were very much excited. Our women were crying and even some of the men cried, because it was terrible and they could do nothing. Afterwhile the Wasichus came and gave us things to tie around us so that we could float. I did not put on the one they gave me. I did not want to float. Instead, I dressed for death, putting on my best clothes that I wore in the show, and then I sang my death song. Others dressed for death too, and sang, because if it was the end of our lives and we could do nothing, we wanted to die brave. We could not fight this that was going to kill us, but we could die so that our spirit relatives would not be ashamed of us. It was harder for us because we were all so sick. Everything we had eaten came right up, and then it kept on trying to come up when there was nothing there.

We did not sleep at all, and in the morning the water looked like mountains, but the wind was not so strong. Some of the bison and elk that we had with us for the show died that day, and the Wasichus threw them in the water. When I saw the poor bison thrown over, I felt like crying, because I thought right there they were throwing part of the power of my people away.

After we had been on the fire-boat a long while, we could see many houses and then many other fire-boats tied close together along the bank. We thought

now we could get off very soon, but we could not. There was a little fire-boat that had come through the gate of waters and it stopped beside us, and the people on it looked at everything on our fire-boat before we could get off. We went very slowly nearly all day, I think, and afterwhile we came to where there were many, many houses close together, and more fire-boats than could be counted. These houses were different from what we had seen before. The Wasichus kept us on the fire-boat all night and then they unloaded us, and took us to a place where the show was going to be. The name of this very big town was London. We were on land now, but we still felt dizzy as though we were still on water, and at first it was hard to walk.

We stayed in this place six moons; and many, many people came to see the show.

One day we were told that Majesty was coming. I did not know what that was at first, but I learned afterward. It was Grandmother England (Queen Victoria), who owned Grandmother's Land where we lived awhile after the Wasichus murdered Crazy Horse.

She came to the show in a big shining wagon, and there were soldiers on both sides of her, and many other shining wagons came too. That day other people could not come to the show—just Grandmother England and some people who came with her.

Sometimes we had to shoot in the show, but this time we did not shoot at all. We danced and sang, and I was one of the dancers chosen to do this for the Grandmother, because I was young and limber then and could dance many ways. We stood right in front of Grandmother England. She was little but fat and we liked her, because she was good to us.

187

After we had danced, she spoke to us. She said something like this: "I am sixty-seven years old. All over the world I have seen all kinds of people; but to-day I have seen the best-looking people I know. If you belonged to me, I would not let them take you around in a show like this." She said other good things too, and then she said we must come to see her, because she had come to see us. She shook hands with all of us. Her hand was very little and soft. We gave a big cheer for her, and then the shining wagons came in and she got into one of them and they all went away.

In about a half-moon after that we went to see the Grandmother. They put us in some of those shining wagons and took us to a very beautiful place where there was a very big house with sharp, pointed towers on it. There were many seats built high in a circle, and these were just full of Wasichus who were all pounding their heels and yelling: "Jubilee! Jubilee! Jubilee!" I never heard what this meant.

They put us together in a certain place at the bottom of the seats. First there appeared a beautiful black wagon with two black horses, and it went all around the show place. I heard that the Grandmother's grandson, a little boy, was in that wagon. Next came a beautiful black wagon with four gray horses. On each of the two right hand horses there was a rider, and a man walked, holding the front left hand horse. I heard that some of Grandmother's relatives were in this wagon. Next came eight buckskin horses, two by two, pulling a shining black wagon. There was a rider on each right-hand horse and a man walked, holding the front left hand horse. There were soldiers, with bayonets, facing outward all around this wagon. Now all the people in the

seats were roaring and yelling "Jubilee!" and "Victoria!" Then we saw Grandmother England again. She was sitting in the back of the wagon and two women sat in the front, facing her. Her dress was all shining and her hat was all shining and her wagon was all shining and so were the horses. She looked like a fire coming.

Afterward I heard that there was yellow and white metal all over the horses and the wagon.

When she came to where we were, her wagon stopped and she stood up. Then all those people stood up and roared and bowed to her; but she bowed to us. We sent up a great cry and our women made the tremolo. The people in the crowd were so excited that we heard some of them got sick and fell over. Then when it was quiet, we sang a song to the Grandmother.

That was a very happy time.

We liked Grandmother England, because we could see that she was a fine woman, and she was good to us. Maybe if she had been our Grandmother, it would have been better for our people.

XX

The Spirit Journey

Yes, that was a happy time; but it was all over. We went to Manchester and had a show there for several moons.

When the show was going to leave very early next morning, three other young men and myself got lost in Manchester, and the fire-boat went away without us. We could not talk the Wasichu language and we did not know what to do, so we just roamed around. Afterwhile we found two other Lakotas who had been left behind, and one of these could talk English. He said if we went to London we could get money in another show that was there, and then we could go home. We were all sick to go home. So the English-talker got some tickets with the money we all had together, and we went to London on the iron road.

The show was called Mexican Joe. It was a small show, but they gave us a dollar every day for being in it. After we had been in London awhile, Mexican Joe took us to Paris, and we had a show there a long while. There was a Wasichu girl who came to the show very often. She liked me and took me home to see her father and mother. They liked me

too and were good to me. I could not talk their language. I made signs, and the girl learned a few Lakota words.

From Paris, we went into Germany and from there to a place where the earth was burning. There was a tall butte, shaped at the top like a tepee, and it was burning up there. I heard that a long time ago a big town and many people disappeared in the earth there.

I was more and more sick to go home all the time now, because it had been two winters since I went away. I could not think of anything else, and after-while this made me really sick, but I thought I would have to stay with the show until I could get money enough to go home.

Mexican Joe took us back to Paris, but I could not be in the show because I was so sick now. The girl I told you about took me home to her father and mother, and they made me well. Then one morning I did go home for awhile.

That morning I had on Wasichu clothes and shoes and everything. The only difference was that my hair was long. It was not braided, just hanging back over my shoulders. I was feeling well and we were just sitting down to eat the first meal. This girl-friend of mine was sitting by me, and her mother and father and two sisters were sitting down too.

As we sat there, I looked up at the roof and it seemed to be moving. The house was going around up at the top, and stretching upward as it went around. I could see that we were all rising fast with the whole house, and it was turning around as it 'rose. Then a cloud was coming down as we 'rose, and suddenly I was on it and the other people and the house were falling back away from me.

Then I was alone on this cloud, and it was going fast. I clung to it hard, because I was afraid I might fall off. Far down below I could see houses and towns and green land and streams, and it all looked flat. Then I was right over the big water. I was not afraid any more, because, by now, I knew I was going home. It was dark, and then it was light again, and I could see a big town below me, and I knew it was the one where we first got on the big fire-boat, and that I was in my own country again. I was very happy now. The cloud and I kept on going very fast, and I could see towns and streams and towns and green land. Then I began to recognize the country below me. I saw the Missouri River. Then I saw far off the Black Hills and the center of the world where the spirits had taken me in my great vision.

Then I was right over Pine Ridge, and the cloud stopped. I looked down and could not understand what I saw, because it seemed that nearly all of my people of the different bands were gathered together there in a big camp. I saw my father's and mother's tepee. They were outside, and she was cooking. I wanted to jump off the cloud and be with them, but I was afraid it would kill me. While I was looking down, my mother looked up, and I felt sure she saw me. But just then the cloud started back, going very fast. I was very sad, but I could not get off. There were streams and green land and towns going backward very fast below me. Soon the cloud and I were going right over the very big town again. Then there was only water under me, and the night came without stars; and I was all alone in a black world and I was crying. But afterwhile some light began to peep in far ahead of me. Then I saw earth be-

neath me and towns and green land and houses all flying backwards. Soon the cloud stopped over a big town, and a house began coming up toward me, turning around and around as it came. When it touched the cloud, it caught me and began to drop down, turning around and around with me.

It touched the ground, and as it touched I heard the girl's voice, and then other voices of frightened people.

Then I was lying on my back in bed and the girl and her father and her mother and her two sisters and a doctor were looking at me in a queer way, as though they were frightened. The English-talker came from the show and he told me how it was. While I was sitting at breakfast, they said, I had looked up and smiled, and then I had fallen like dead out of my chair. I had been dead three days, except that once in awhile I would breathe just a little. Often they said they could not feel my heart at all. They were sure I would soon be really dead, and they were getting ready to buy my coffin.

Maybe if I had not come back to life that time, they would have given me a good coffin; but as it is, I think it will be only a box.

I did not tell the people where I had been, because I knew they could not believe me.

A few days after that, these people heard that Pahuska was in town again. So they took me to where he had his show, and he was glad to see me. He had all his people give me three cheers. Then he asked me if I wanted to be in the show or if I wanted to go home. I told him I was sick to go home. So he said he would fix that. He gave me a ticket and ninety dollars. Then he gave me a big dinner. Pahuska had a strong heart. Afterwhile a

BLACK ELK SPEAKS

policeman came and told me to get my things. He
took me to the iron road, and in the morning I was
by the big water and they put me on another big
fire-boat. We were on the water eight days. I was
sick part of the time, but I was not sad, because I
was going home.

When the fire-boat was back at the big town in
my own country again, I started right away on the
iron road.

It was early in the morning when we came to
Rushville. There were no Lakotas there at all, but
there was a covered wagon with mules starting out
for Pine Ridge, so I rode in the wagon.

When I got to Pine Ridge, everything was just as
I had seen it from the cloud. All the Lakotas were
there, as I had seen them, because that was the
year of the treaty (1889) when the Wasichus bought
some more of our land—all that was between the
Smoky Earth (the White) and Good River (the
Cheyenne). I had been away nearly three years and
knew nothing about this foolish thing until then.

My mother's tepee was right where I had seen it
when I looked down from the cloud, and other peo-
ple were camped exactly where I saw them.

My parents were in great joy to see me and my
mother cried because she was so happy. I cried too.
I was supposed to be a man now, but the tears came
out anyway. My mother told me she had dreamed
one night in her sleep that I had come back on a
cloud, but could not stay. So I told her about my
vision.

194

XXI

The Messiah

There was hunger among my people before I went away across the big water, because the Wasichus did not give us all the food they promised in the Black Hills treaty. They made that treaty themselves; our people did not want it and did not make it. Yet the Wasichus who made it had given us less than half as much as they promised. So the people were hungry before I went away.

But it was worse when I came back. My people looked pitiful. There was a big drouth, and the rivers and creeks seemed to be dying. Nothing would grow that the people had planted, and the Wasichus had been sending less cattle and other food than ever before. The Wasichus had slaughtered all the bison and shut us up in pens. It looked as though we might all starve to death. We could not eat lies, and there was nothing we could do.

And now the Wasichus had made another treaty to take away from us about half the land we had left. Our people did not want this treaty either, but Three Stars[1] came and made the treaty just the

[1] General Crook headed the commission that arranged the treaty of 1889.

same, because the Wasichus wanted our land between the Smoky Earth and the Good River. So the flood of Wasichus, dirty with bad deeds, gnawed away half of the island that was left to us. When Three Stars came to kill us on the Rosebud, Crazy Horse whipped him and drove him back. But when he came this time without any soldiers, he whipped us and drove us back. We were penned up and could do nothing.

All the time I was away from home across the big water, my power was gone, and I was like a dead man moving around most of the time. I could hardly remember my vision, and when I did remember, it seemed like a dim dream.

Just after I came back, some people asked me to cure a sick person, and I was afraid the power would not come back to me; but it did. So I went on helping the sick, and there were many, for the measles had come among the people who were already weak because of hunger. There were more sick people that winter when the whooping cough came and killed little children who did not have enough to eat.

So it was. Our people were pitiful and in despair.

But early that summer when I came back from across the big water (1889) strange news had come from the west, and the people had been talking and talking about it. They were talking about it when I came home, and that was the first I had heard of it. This news came to the Ogalalas first of all, and I heard that it came to us from the Shoshones and Blue Clouds (Arapahoes). Some believed it and some did not believe. It was hard to believe; and when I first heard of it, I thought it was only foolish talk that somebody had started somewhere. This

news said that out yonder in the west at a place
near where the great mountains (The Sierras) stand
before you come to the big water, there was a sacred
man among the Paiūtes who had talked to the Great
Spirit in a vision, and the Great Spirit had told him
how to save the Indian peoples and make the Wasi-
chus disappear and bring back all the bison and the
people who were dead and how there would be a
new earth. Before I came back, the people had
got together to talk about this and they had sent
three men, Good Thunder, Brave Bear and Yellow
Breast, to see this sacred man with their own eyes
and learn if the story about him was true. So these
three men had made the long journey west, and in
the fall after I came home, they returned to the
Ogalalas with wonderful things to tell.

There was a big meeting at the head of White
Clay Creek, not far from Pine Ridge, when they
came back, but I did not go over there to hear,
because I did not yet believe. I thought maybe it
was only the despair that made people believe, just
as a man who is starving may dream of plenty
of everything good to eat.

I did not go over to the meeting, but I heard all
they had to tell. These three men all said the same
thing, and they were good men. They said that they
traveled far until they came to a great flat valley[2]
near the last great mountains before the big water,
and there they saw the Wanekia,[3] who was the son
of the Great Spirit, and they talked to him. Wasichus
called him Jack Wilson, but his name was Wovoka.
He told them that there was another world coming,

[2] Mason Valley, Nevada.
[3] "One Who Makes Live."

just like a cloud. It would come in a whirlwind out of the west and would crush out everything on this world, which was old and dying. In that other world there was plenty of meat, just like old times; and in that world all the dead Indians were alive, and all the bison that had ever been killed were roaming around again.

This sacred man gave some sacred red paint and two eagle feathers to Good Thunder. The people must put this paint on their faces and they must dance a ghost dance that the sacred man taught to Good Thunder, Yellow Breast, and Brave Bear. If they did this, they could get on this other world when it came, and the Wasichus would not be able to get on, and so they would disappear. When he gave the two eagle feathers to Good Thunder, the sacred man said: "Receive these eagle feathers and behold them, for my father will cause these to bring your people back to him."

This was all that was heard the whole winter.

When I heard this about the red paint and the eagle feathers and about bringing the people back to the Great Spirit, it made me think hard. I had had a great vision that was to bring the people back into the nation's hoop, and maybe this sacred man had had the same vision and it was going to come true, so that the people would get back on the red road. Maybe I was not meant to do this myself, but if I helped with the power that was given me, the tree might bloom again and the people prosper. This was in my mind all that winter, but I did not know what vision the sacred man out there had seen, and I wished I could talk to him and find out. This was sitting deeper in my mind every day, and

it was a very bad winter, with mucn hunger and sickness.

My father died in the first part of the winter from the bad sickness that many people had. This made me very sad. Everything good seemed to be going away. My younger brother and sister had died before I came home, and now I was fatherless in this world. But I still had my mother. I was working in a store for the Wasichus so that I could get something for her to eat, and I just kept on working there and thinking about what Good Thunder, Yellow Breast, and Brave Bear had told; but I did not feel sure yet.

During that winter the people wanted to hear some more about this sacred man and the new world coming, so they sent more men out there to learn what they could. Good Thunder and Yellow Breast, with two others, went from Pine Ridge. Some went with them from other agencies, and two of these were Kicking Bear and Short Bull. News came back from these men as they traveled west, and it seemed that everywhere people believed all that we had heard, and more. Letters came back telling us this. I kept on working in the store and helping sick people with my power.

Then it was spring (1890), and I heard that these men had all come back from the west and that they said it was all true. I did not go to this meeting either, but I heard the gossip that was everywhere now, and people said it was really the son of the Great Spirit who was out there; that when he came to the Wasichus a long time ago, they had killed him; but he was coming to the Indians this time, and there would not be any Wasichus in the new world that would come like a cloud in a whirl-wind and crush out the old earth that was dying.

This they said would happen after one more winter, when the grasses were appearing (1891).

I heard many wonderful things about the Wanekia that these men had seen and heard, and they were good men. He could make animals talk, and once while they were with him he made a spirit vision, and they all saw it. They saw a big water, and beyond it was a beautiful green land where all the Indians that had ever lived and the bison and the other animals were all coming home together. Then the Wanekia, they said, made the vision go out, because it was not yet time for this to happen. After another winter it would happen, when the grasses were appearing.

And once, they said, the Wanekia held out his hat for them to look into; and when they did this, all but one saw there the whole world and all that was wonderful. But that one could see only the inside of the hat, they said.

Good Thunder himself told me that, with the power of the Wanekia, he had gone to a bison skin tepee; and there his son, who had been dead a long time, was living with his wife, and they had a long talk together.

This was not like my great vision, and I just went on working in the store. I was puzzled and did not know what to think.

Afterwhile I heard that north of Pine Ridge at the head of Cheyenne Creek, Kicking Bear had held the first ghost dance, and that people who danced had seen their dead relatives and talked to them. The next thing I heard was that they were dancing on Wounded Knee Creek just below Manderson.

I did not believe yet, but I wanted to find out things, because all this was sitting more and more

strongly in my heart since my father died. Some-
thing seemed to tell me to go and see. For awhile
I kept from going, but at last I could not any more.
So I got on my horse and went to this ghost dance
on Wounded Knee Creek below Manderson.

I was surprised, and could hardly believe what I
saw; because so much of my vision seemed to be in
it. The dancers, both women and men, were holding
hands in a big circle, and in the center of the circle
they had a tree painted red with most of its branches
cut off and some dead leaves on it. This was exactly
like the part of my vision where the holy tree was
dying, and the circle of the men and women holding
hands was like the sacred hoop that should have
power to make the tree to bloom again. I saw too
that the sacred articles the people had offered were
scarlet, as in my vision, and all their faces were
painted red. Also, they used the pipe and the eagle
feathers. I sat there looking on and feeling sad. It
all seemed to be from my great vision somehow
and I had done nothing yet to make the tree to
bloom.

Then all at once great happiness overcame me,
and it all took hold of me right there. This was to
remind me to get to work at once and help to
bring my people back into the sacred hoop, that
they might again walk the red road in a sacred
manner pleasing to the Powers of the Universe that
are One Power. I remembered how the spirits had
taken me to the center of the earth and shown me
the good things, and how my people should prosper.
I remembered how the Six Grandfathers had told me
that through their power I should make my people
live and the holy tree should bloom. I believed my

vision was coming true at last, and happiness over-
came me.

When I went to the dance, I went only to see
and to learn what the people believed; but now I
was going to stay and use the power that had been
given me. The dance was over for that day, but
they would dance again next day, and I would dance
with them.

XXII

Visions of the Other World

So I dressed myself in a sacred manner, and before the dance began next morning I went among the people who were standing around the withered tree. Good Thunder, who was a relative of my father and later married my mother, put his arms around me and took me to the sacred tree that had not bloomed, and there he offered up a prayer for me. He said: "Father, Great Spirit, behold this boy! Your ways he shall see!" Then he began to cry.

I thought of my father and my brother and sister who had left us, and I could not keep the tears from running out of my eyes. I raised my face up to keep them back, but they came out just the same. I cried with my whole heart, and while I cried I thought of my people in despair. I thought of my vision, and how it was promised me that my people should have a place in this earth where they could be happy every day. I thought of them on the wrong road now, but maybe they could be brought back into the hoop again and to the good road.

Under the tree that never bloomed I stood and cried because it had withered away. With tears on

my face I asked the Great Spirit to give it life and
leaves and singing birds, as in my vision.

Then there came a strong shivering all over my
body, and I knew that the power was in me.

Good Thunder now took one of my arms, Kick-
ing Bear the other, and we began to dance. The song
we sang was like this:

"Who do you think he is that comes?
It is one who seeks his mother!"

It was what the dead would sing when entering the
other world and looking for their relatives who had
gone there before them.

As I danced, with Good Thunder and Kicking
Bear holding my arms between them, I had the
queer feeling that I knew and I seemed to be lifted
clear off the ground. I did not have a vision all that
first day. That night I thought about the other world
and that the Wanekia himself was with my people
there and maybe the holy tree of my vision was
really blooming yonder right then, and that it was
there my vision had already come true. From the
center of the earth I had been shown all good and
beautiful things in a great circle of peace, and maybe
this land of my vision was where all my people were
going, and there they would live and prosper where
no Wasichus were or could ever be.

Before we started dancing next day, Kicking Bear
offered a prayer, saying: "Father, Great Spirit, be-
hold these people! They shall go forth to-day to see
their relatives, and yonder they shall be happy, day
after day, and their happiness will not end."

Then we began dancing, and most of the people
wailed and cried as they danced, holding hands in

a circle; but some of them laughed with happiness. Now and then some one would fall down like dead, and others would go staggering around and panting before they would fall. While they were lying there like dead they were having visions, and we kept on dancing and singing, and many were crying for the old way of living and that the old religion might be with them again.

After awhile I began to feel very queer. First, my legs seemed to be full of ants. I was dancing with my eyes closed, as the others did. Suddenly it seemed that I was swinging off the ground and not touching it any longer. The queer feeling came up from my legs and was in my heart now. It seemed I would glide forward like a swing, and then glide back again in longer and longer swoops. There was no fear with this, just a growing happiness.

I must have fallen down, but I felt as though I had fallen off a swing when it was going forward, and I was floating head first through the air. My arms were stretched out, and all I saw at first was a single eagle feather right in front of me. Then the feather was a spotted eagle dancing on ahead of me with his wings fluttering, and he was making the shrill whistle that is his. My body did not move at all, but I looked ahead and floated fast toward where I looked.

There was a ridge right in front of me, and I thought I was going to run into it, but I went right over it. On the other side of the ridge I could see a beautiful land where many, many people were camping in a great circle. I could see that they were happy and had plenty. Everywhere there were drying racks full of meat. The air was clear and beautiful with a living light that was everywhere. All around

the circle, feeding on the green, green grass, were fat and happy horses; and animals of all kinds were scattered all over the green hills, and singing hunters were returning with their meat.

I floated over the tepees and began to come down feet first at the center of the hoop where I could see a beautiful tree all green and full of flowers. When I touched the ground, two men were coming toward me, and they wore holy shirts made and painted in a certain way. They came to me and said: "It is not yet time to see your father, who is happy. You have work to do. We will give you something that you shall carry back to your people, and with it they shall come to see their loved ones."

I knew it was the way their holy shirts were made that they wanted me to take back. They told me to return at once, and then I was out in the air again, floating fast as before. When I came right over the dancing place, the people were still dancing, but it seemed they were not making any sound. I had hoped to see the withered tree in bloom, but it was dead.

Then I fell back into my body, and as I did this I heard voices all around and above me, and I was sitting on the ground. Many were crowding around, asking me what vision I had seen. I told them just what I had seen, and what I brought back was the memory of the holy shirts the two men wore.

That evening some of us got together at Big Road's tepee and decided to use the ghost shirts I had seen. So the next day I made ghost shirts all day long and painted them in the sacred manner of my vision. As I made these shirts, I thought how in my vision everything was like old times and the tree was flowering, but when I came back the tree was dead.

And I thought that if this world would do as the vision teaches, the tree could bloom here too.

I made the first shirt for Afraid-of-Hawk and the second for the son of Big Road.

In the evening I made a sacred stick like that I had seen in my first vision and painted it red with the sacred paint of the Wanekia. On the top of it I tied one eagle feather, and this I carried in the dance after that, wearing the holy shirt as I had seen it.

Because of my vision and the power they knew I had, I was asked to lead the dance next morning. We all stood in a straight line, facing the west, and I prayed: "Father, Great Spirit, behold me! The nation that I have is in despair. The new earth you promised you have shown me. Let my nation also behold it."

After the prayer we stood with our right hands raised to the west, and we all began to weep, and right there, as they wept, some of them fainted before the dance began.

As we were dancing I had the same queer feeling I had before, as though my feet were off the earth and swinging. Kicking Bear and Good Thunder were holding my arms. Afterwhile it seemed they let go of me, and once more I floated head first, face down, with arms extended, and the spotted eagle was dancing there ahead of me again, and I could hear his shrill whistle and his scream.

I saw the ridge again, and as I neared it there was a deep, rumbling sound, and out of it there leaped a flame. But I glided right over it. There were six villages ahead of me in the beautiful land that was all clear and green in living light. Over these in turn I glided, coming down on the south

207

side of the sixth village. And as I touched the ground, twelve men were coming towards me, and they said: "Our Father, the two-legged chief, you shall see!"

Then they led me to the center of the circle where once more I saw the holy tree all full of leaves and blooming.

But that was not all I saw. Against the tree there was a man standing with arms held wide in front of him. I looked hard at him, and I could not tell what people he came from. He was not a Wasichu and he was not an Indian. His hair was long and hanging loose, and on the left side of his head he wore an eagle feather. His body was strong and good to see, and it was painted red. I tried to recognize him, but I could not make him out. He was a very fine-looking man. While I was staring hard at him, his body began to change and became very beautiful with all colors of light, and around him there was light. He spoke like singing: "My life is such that all earthly beings and growing things belong to me. Your father, the Great Spirit, has said this. You too must say this."

Then he went out like a light in a wind.

The twelve men who were there spoke: "Behold them! Your nation's life shall be such!"

I saw again how beautiful the day was—the sky all blue and full of yellow light above the greening earth. And I saw that all the people were beautiful and young. There were no old ones there, nor children either—just people of about one age, and beautiful.

Then there were twelve women who stood in front of me and spoke: "Behold them! Their way of life you shall take back to earth." When they had spo-

ken, I heard singing in the west, and I learned the song I heard.

Then one of the twelve men took two sticks, one painted white and one red, and, thrusting them in the ground, he said: "Take these! You shall depend upon them. Make haste!"

I started to walk, and it seemed as though a strong wind went under me and picked me up. I was in the air, with outstretched arms, and floating fast. There was a fearful dark river that I had to go over, and I was afraid. It rushed and roared and was full of angry foam. Then I looked down and saw many men and women who were trying to cross the dark and fearful river, but they could not. Weeping, they looked up to me and cried: "Help us!" But I could not stop gliding, for it was as though a great wind were under me.

Then I saw my earthly people again at the dancing place, and fell back into my body lying there. And I was sitting up, and people were crowding around me to ask what vision I had seen.

I told my vision through songs, and the older men explained them to the others. I sang a song, the words of which were those the Wanekia spoke under the flowering tree, and the air of it was that which I heard in the West after the twelve women had spoken. I sang it four times, and the fourth time all the people began to weep together because the Wasichus had taken the beautiful world away from us.

I thought and thought about this vision. The six villages seemed to represent the Six Grandfathers that I had seen long ago in the Flaming Rainbow Tepee, and I had gone to the sixth village, which was for the Sixth Grandfather, the Spirit of the Earth,

because I was to stand for him in the world. I wondered if the Wanekia might be the red man of my great vision, who turned into a bison, and then into the four-rayed herb, the daybreak-star herb of understanding. I thought the twelve men and twelve women were for the moons of the year.

XXIII

Bad Trouble Coming

While these things were happening, the summer (1890) was getting old. I did not then know all that was going on at other places, but some things I heard, and much more I heard later.

When Good Thunder and Kicking Bear came back in the spring from seeing the Wanekia, the Wasichus at Pine Ridge put them in prison awhile, and then let them go. This showed the Wasichus were afraid of something. In the Moon of Black Cherries (August) many people were dancing at No Water's Camp on Clay Creek, and the agent came and told them to stop dancing. They would not stop, and they said they would fight for their religion if they had to do it. The agent went away, and they kept on dancing. They called him Young-Man-Afraid-of-Lakotas.

Later, I heard that the Brules were dancing over east of us; and then I heard that Big Foot's people were dancing on the Good River reservation; also that Kicking Bear had gone to Sitting Bull's camp on Grand River, and that the people were dancing there too. Word came to us that the Indians were beginning to dance everywhere.

211

The people were hungry and in despair, and many believed in the good new world that was coming. The Wasichus gave us less than half the beef cattle they promised us in the treaty, and these cattle were very poor. For a while our people would not take the cattle, because there were so few of them and they were so poor. But afterwhile they had to take them or starve to death. So we got more lies than cattle, and we could not eat lies. When the agent told the people to quit dancing, their hearts were bad.

From the dancing on Wounded Knee I went over to the Brules, who were camping on Cut Meat Creek at this time, and I took with me six shirts like those I had seen the twelve men wearing in my vision, and six dresses like the twelve women wore. I gave these to the Brules and they made others for themselves.

We danced there, and another vision came to me. I saw a Flaming Rainbow, like the one I had seen in my first great vision. Below the rainbow was a tepee made of cloud. Over me there was a spotted eagle soaring, and he said to me: "Remember this." That was all I saw and heard.

I have thought much about this since, and I have thought that this was where I made my great mistake. I had had a very great vision, and I should have depended only upon that to guide me to the good. But I followed the lesser visions that had come to me while dancing on Wounded Knee Creek. The vision of the Flaming Rainbow was to warn me, maybe; and I did not understand. I did not depend upon the great vision as I should have done; I depended upon the two sticks that I had seen in the lesser vision. It is hard to follow one great vision in

this world of darkness and of many changing shadows. Among those shadows men get lost.

When I came back from the Brules, the weather was getting cold. Many of the Brules came along when I came back, and joined the Ogalalas in the dancing on Wounded Knee. We heard that there were soldiers at Pine Ridge and that others were coming all the time. Then one morning we heard that the soldiers were marching toward us, so we broke camp and moved west to Grass Creek. From there we went to White Clay and camped awhile and danced.

There came to us Fire Thunder, Red Wound and Young American Horse with a message from the soldiers that this matter of the ghost dance must be looked into, and that there should be rulings over it; and that they did not mean to take the dance away from us. But could we believe anything the Wasichus ever said to us? They spoke with forked tongues.

We moved in closer to Pine Ridge and camped. Many soldiers were there now, and what were they there for?

There was a big meeting with the agent, but I did not go to hear. He made a ruling that we could dance three days every moon, and the rest of the time we should go and make a living for ourselves somehow. He did not say how we could do that. But the people agreed to this.

The next day, while I was sitting in a tepee with Good Thunder, a policeman came to us and said: "I was not sent here, but I came for your good to tell you what I have heard—that they are going to arrest you two."

Good Thunder thought we ought to go to the

Brules, who had a big camp on Wounded Knee below Manderson. So that evening we saddled and started. We came through Pepper Creek and White Horse Creek to Wounded Knee and followed it down to the Brule camp. They were glad to see us.

In the morning the crier went around and called a meeting. I spoke to the Brules, and this is what I said: "My relatives, there is a certain thing that we have done. From that certain sacred thing, we have had visions. In those visions we have seen, and also we have heard, that our relatives who have gone before us are in the Other World that has been revealed to us, and that we too shall go there. They are right now with the Wanekia. If the Wasichus want to fight us, let them do it. Have in your minds a strong desire, and take courage. We must depend upon the departed ones who are in the new world that is coming."

More Brules came there from Porcupine and Medicine Root creeks, and we all broke camp, moving down the Wounded Knee to Smoky Earth River (the White). There a Black Robe (Catholic Priest) came and tried to coax us to return. Our people told him that Wasichu promises were no good; that everything they had promised was a lie. Only a few Ogalalas turned back with the Black Robe. He was a good man and he was badly wounded that winter in the butchering of Big Foot's band. He was a very good man, and not like the other Wasichus.[1]

From Smoky Earth River we moved to High Pockets' place southwest of the Top of the Badlands.[2] While we were there, American Horse and

[1] This was Father Craft.

[2] Cuny Table, a high plateau in the midst of the Badlands.

Fast Thunder came to us. They were both chiefs, and they came to bring us in to Pine Ridge. We had to obey. The Brules would not obey and tried to keep us from going. They struck us, and there was quite a struggle for a while; but we went anyway, because we had to go. Kicking Bear stayed with the Brules that time, but he came in to Pine Ridge a little later. A very few of the Brules went along with us.

We camped on White River, then on White Clay, then on Cheyenne Creek north of Pine Ridge. Most of the Ogalalas were camping near there too.

It was about this time that bad news came to us from the north. We heard that some policemen from Standing Rock had gone to arrest Sitting Bull on Grand River, and that he would not let them take him; so there was a fight, and they killed him.

It was now near the end of the Moon of Popping Trees, and I was twenty-seven years old (December, 1890). We heard that Big Foot was coming down from the Badlands with nearly four hundred people. Some of these were from Sitting Bull's band. They had run away when Sitting Bull was killed, and joined Big Foot on Good River. There were only about a hundred warriors in this band, and all the others were women and children and some old men. They were all starving and freezing, and Big Foot was so sick that they had to bring him along in a pony drag.[3] They had all run away to hide in the Badlands, and they were coming in now because they were starving and freezing. When they crossed Smoky Earth River, they followed up Medicine Root Creek to its head. Soldiers were over there looking for them. The soldiers had everything and were not

[3] He was very ill with pneumonia.

freezing and starving. Near Porcupine Butte the soldiers came up to the Big Foots, and they surrendered and went along with the soldiers to Wounded Knee Creek where the Brenan store is now.

It was in the evening when we heard that the Big Foots were camped over there with the soldiers, about fifteen miles by the old road from where we were. It was the next morning (December 29, 1890) that something terrible happened.

XXIV

The Butchering
at Wounded Knee

That evening before it happened, I went in to Pine
Ridge and heard these things, and while I was there,
soldiers started for where the Big Foots were. These
made about five hundred soldiers that were there next
morning. When I saw them starting I felt that some-
thing terrible was going to happen. That night I
could hardly sleep at all. I walked around most of
the night.

In the morning I went out after my horses, and
while I was out I heard shooting off toward the east,
and I knew from the sound that it must be wagon-
guns (cannon) going off. The sounds went right
through my body, and I felt that something terrible
would happen.

When I reached camp with the horses, a man rode
up to me and said: "Hey-hey-hey! The people that
are coming are fired on! I know it!"

I saddled up my buckskin and put on my sacred
shirt. It was one I had made to be worn by no one
but myself. It had a spotted eagle outstretched on
the back of it, and the daybreak star was on the

217

left shoulder, because when facing south that shoulder is toward the east. Across the breast, from the left shoulder to the right hip, was the flaming rainbow, and there was another rainbow around the neck, like a necklace, with a star at the bottom. At each shoulder, elbow, and wrist was an eagle feather; and over the whole shirt were red streaks of lightning. You will see that this was from my great vision, and you will know how it protected me that day.

I painted my face all red, and in my hair I put one eagle feather for the One Above.

It did not take me long to get ready, for I could still hear the shooting over there.

I started out alone on the old road that ran across the hills to Wounded Knee. I had no gun. I carried only the sacred bow of the west that I had seen in my great vision. I had gone only a little way when a band of young men came galloping after me. The first two who came up were Loves War and Iron Wasichu. I asked what they were going to do, and they said they were just going to see where the shooting was. Then others were coming up, and some older men.

We rode fast, and there were about twenty of us now. The shooting was getting louder. A horseback from over there came galloping very fast toward us, and he said: "Hey-hey-hey! They have murdered them!" Then he whipped his horse and rode away faster toward Pine Ridge.

In a little while we had come to the top of the ridge where, looking to the east, you can see for the first time the monument and the burying ground on the little hill where the church is. That is where the terrible thing started. Just south of the burying

ground on the little hill a deep dry gulch runs about east and west, very crooked, and it rises westward to nearly the top of the ridge where we were. It had no name, but the Wasichus sometimes call it Battle Creek now. We stopped on the ridge not far from the head of the dry gulch. Wagon guns were still going off over there on the little hill, and they were going off again where they hit along the gulch. There was much shooting down yonder, and there were many cries, and we could see cavalrymen scattered over the hills ahead of us. Cavalrymen were riding along the gulch and shooting into it, where the women and children were running away and trying to hide in the gullies and the stunted pines.

A little way ahead of us, just below the head of the dry gulch, there were some women and children who were huddled under a clay bank, and some cavalrymen were there pointing guns at them.

We stopped back behind the ridge, and I said to the others: "Take courage. These are our relatives. We will try to get them back." Then we all sang a song which went like this:

"A thunder being nation I am, I have said.
A thunder being nation I am, I have said.
You shall live.
You shall live.
You shall live.
You shall live."

Then I rode over the ridge and the others after me, and we were crying: "Take courage! It is time to fight!" The soldiers who were guarding our relatives shot at us and then ran away fast, and some more cavalrymen on the other side of the gulch did

too. We got our relatives and sent them across the ridge to the northwest where they would be safe.

I had no gun, and when we were charging, I just held the sacred bow out in front of me with my right hand. The bullets did not hit us at all.

We found a little baby lying all alone near the head of the gulch. I could not pick her up just then, but I got her later and some of my people adopted her. I just wrapped her up tighter in a shawl that was around her and left her there. It was a safe place, and I had other work to do.

The soldiers had run eastward over the hills where there were some more soldiers, and they were off their horses and lying down. I told the others to stay back, and I charged upon them holding the sacred bow out toward them with my right hand. They all shot at me, and I could hear bullets all around me, but I ran my horse right close to them, and then swung around. Some soldiers across the gulch began shooting at me too, but I got back to the others and was not hurt at all.

By now many other Lakotas, who had heard the shooting, were coming up from Pine Ridge, and we all charged on the soldiers. They ran eastward toward where the trouble began. We followed down along the dry gulch, and what we saw was terrible. Dead and wounded women and children and little babies were scattered all along there where they had been trying to run away. The soldiers had followed along the gulch, as they ran, and murdered them in there. Sometimes they were in heaps because they had huddled together, and some were scattered all along. Sometimes bunches of them had been killed and torn to pieces where the wagon guns hit

them. I saw a little baby trying to suck its mother, but she was bloody and dead.

There were two little boys at one place in this gulch. They had guns and they had been killing soldiers all by themselves. We could see the soldiers they had killed. The boys were all alone there, and they were not hurt. These were very brave little boys.

When we drove the soldiers back, they dug themselves in, and we were not enough people to drive them out from there. In the evening they marched off up Wounded Knee Creek, and then we saw all that they had done there.

Men and women and children were heaped and scattered all over the flat at the bottom of the little hill where the soldiers had their wagon-guns, and westward up the dry gulch all the way to the high ridge, the dead women and children and babies were scattered.

When I saw this I wished that I had died too, but I was not sorry for the women and children. It was better for them to be happy in the other world, and I wanted to be there too. But before I went there I wanted to have revenge. I thought there might be a day, and we should have revenge.

After the soldiers marched away, I heard from my friend, Dog Chief, how the trouble started, and he was right there by Yellow Bird when it happened. This is the way it was:

In the morning the soldiers began to take all the guns away from the Big Foots, who were camped in the flat below the little hill where the monument and burying ground are now. The people had stacked most of their guns, and even their knives, by the tepee where Big Foot was lying sick. Soldiers were

on the little hill and all around, and there were soldiers across the dry gulch to the south and over east along Wounded Knee Creek too. The people were nearly surrounded, and the wagon-guns were pointing at them.

Some had not yet given up their guns, and so the soldiers were searching all the tepees, throwing things around and poking into everything. There was a man called Yellow Bird, and he and another man were standing in front of the tepee where Big Foot was lying sick. They had white sheets around and over them, with eyeholes to look through, and they had guns under these. An officer came to search them. He took the other man's gun, and then started to take Yellow Bird's. But Yellow Bird would not let go. He wrestled with the officer, and while they were wrestling, the gun went off and killed the officer. Wasichus and some others have said he meant to do this, but Dog Chief was standing right there, and he told me it was not so. As soon as the gun went off, Dog Chief told me, an officer shot and killed Big Foot who was lying sick inside the tepee.

Then suddenly nobody knew what was happening, except that the soldiers were all shooting and the wagon-guns began going off right in among the people.

Many were shot down right there. The women and children ran into the gulch and up west, dropping all the time, for the soldiers shot them as they ran. There were only about a hundred warriors and there were nearly five hundred soldiers. The warriors rushed to where they had piled their guns and knives. They fought soldiers with only their hands until they got their guns.

Dog Chief saw Yellow Bird run into a tepee with

his gun, and from there he killed soldiers until the tepee caught fire. Then he died full of bullets.

It was a good winter day when all this happened. The sun was shining. But after the soldiers marched away from their dirty work, a heavy snow began to fall. The wind came up in the night. There was a big blizzard, and it grew very cold. The snow drifted deep in the crooked gulch, and it was one long grave of butchered women and children and babies, who had never done any harm and were only trying to run away.

XXV

The End of the Dream

After the soldiers marched away, Red Crow and I
started back toward Pine Ridge together, and I took
the little baby that I told you about. Red Crow had
one too.

We were going back to Pine Ridge, because we
thought there was peace back home; but it was not
so. While we were gone, there was a fight around the
Agency, and our people had all gone away. They
had gone away so fast that they left all the tepees
standing.

It was nearly dark when we passed north of Pine
Ridge where the hospital is now, and some soldiers
shot at us, but did not hit us. We rode into the
camp, and it was all empty. We were very hungry
because we had not eaten anything since early morn-
ing, so we peeped into the tepees until we saw where
there was a pot with papa (dried meat) cooked in
it. We sat down in there and began to eat. While
we were doing this, the soldiers shot at the tepee, and
a bullet struck right between Red Crow and me. It
threw dust in the soup, but we kept right on eating
until we had our fill. Then we took the babies and
got on our horses and rode away. If that bullet had

only killed me, then I could have died with papa in my mouth.

The people had fled down Clay Creek, and we followed their trail. It was dark now, and late in the night we came to where they were camped without any tepees. They were just sitting by little fires, and the snow was beginning to blow. We rode in among them and I heard my mother's voice. She was singing a death song for me, because she felt sure I had died over there. She was so glad to see me that she cried and cried.

Women who had milk fed the little babies that Red Crow and I brought with us.

I think nobody but the little children slept any that night. The snow blew and we had no tepees.

When it was getting light, a war party went out and I went along; but this time I took a gun with me. When I started out the day before to Wounded Knee, I took only my sacred bow, which was not made to shoot with; because I was a little in doubt about the Wanekia religion at that time, and I did not really want to kill anybody because of it.

But I did not feel like that any more. After what I had seen over there, I wanted revenge; I wanted to kill.

We crossed White Clay Creek and followed it up, keeping on the west side. Soon we could hear many guns going off. So we struck west, following a ridge to where the fight was. It was close to the Mission, and there are many bullets in the Mission yet.

From this ridge we could see that the Lakotas were on both sides of the creek and were shooting at soldiers who were coming down the creek. As we looked down, we saw a little ravine, and across this was a big hill. We crossed and rode up the hillside.

They were fighting right there, and a Lakota cried to me: "Black Elk, this is the kind of a day in which to do something great!" I answered: "How!"[1]

Then I got off my horse and rubbed earth on myself, to show the Powers that I was nothing without their help. Then I took my rifle, got on my horse and galloped up to the top of the hill. Right below me the soldiers were shooting, and my people called out to me not to go down there; that there were some good shots among the soldiers and I should get killed for nothing.

But I remembered my great vision, the part where the geese of the north appeared. I depended upon their power. Stretching out my arms with my gun in the right hand, like a goose soaring when it flies low to turn in a change of weather, I made the sound the geese make—br-r-r-p, br-r-r-p, br-r-r-p; and, doing this, I charged. The soldiers saw, and began shooting fast at me. I kept right on with my buckskin running, shot in their faces when I was near, then swung wide and rode back up the hill.

All this time the bullets were buzzing around me and I was not touched. I was not even afraid. It was like being in a dream about shooting. But just as I had reached the very top of the hill, suddenly it was like waking up, and I was afraid. I dropped my arms and quit making the goose cry. Just as I did this, I felt something strike my belt as though someone had hit me there with the back of an ax. I nearly fell out of my saddle, but I managed to hold on, and rode over the hill.

An old man by the name of Protector was there,

[1] Signifying assent.

and he ran up and held me, for now I was falling off
my horse. I will show you where the bullet struck
me sidewise across the belly here (showing a long
deep scar on the abdomen). My insides were coming
out. Protector tore up a blanket in strips and bound
it around me so that my insides would stay in. By
now I was crazy to kill, and I said to Protector:
"Help me on my horse! Let me go over there. It is
a good day to die, so I will go over there!" But Pro-
tector said: "No, young nephew! You must not die
to-day. That would be foolish. Your people need
you. There may be a better day to die." He lifted
me into my saddle and led my horse away down hill.
Then I began to feel very sick.

By now it looked as though the soldiers would
be wiped out, and the Lakotas were fighting harder;
but I heard that, after I left, the black Wasichu sol-
diers came, and the Lakotas had to retreat.

There were many of our children in the Mission,
and the sisters and priests were taking care of them.
I heard there were sisters and priests right in the
battle helping wounded people and praying.

There was a man by the name of Little Soldier
who took charge of me and brought me to where
our people were camped. While we were over at
the Mission Fight, they had fled to the O-ona-
gazhee[2] and were camped on top of it where the
women and children would be safe from soldiers.
Old Hollow Horn was there. He was a very powerful
bear medicine man, and he came over to heal my
wound. In three days I could walk, but I kept a
piece of blanket tied around my belly.

[2] Sheltering place, an elevated plateau in the Badlands,
with precipitous sides, and inaccessible save by one narrow
neck of land easily defended.

It was now nearly the middle of the Moon of
Frost in the Tepee (January). We heard that sol-
diers were on Smoky Earth River and were coming
to attack us in the O-ona-gazhee. They were near
Black Feather's place. So a party of about sixty of
us started on the war-path to find them. My mother
tried to keep me at home, because, although I could
walk and ride a horse, my wound was not all healed
yet. But I would not stay; for, after what I had
seen at Wounded Knee, I wanted a chance to kill
soldiers.

We rode down Grass Creek to Smoky Earth, and
crossed, riding down stream. Soon from the top of a
little hill we saw wagons and cavalry guarding them.
The soldiers were making a corral of their wagons
and getting ready to fight. We got off our horses and
went behind some hills to a little knoll, where we
crept up to look at the camp. Some soldiers were
bringing harnessed horses down to a little creek to
water, and I said to the others: "If you will stay
here and shoot at the soldiers, I will charge over
there and get some good horses." They knew of my
power, so they did this, and I charged on my buck-
skin while the others kept shooting. I got seven of
the horses; but when I started back with these, all
the soldiers saw me and began shooting. They killed
two of my horses, but I brought five back safe and
was not hit. When I was out of range, I caught up
a fine bald-faced bay and turned my buckskin
loose. Then I drove the others back to our party.

By now more cavalry were coming up the river,
a big bunch of them, and there was some hard fight-
ing for a while, because there were not enough of us.
We were fighting and retreating, and all at once I

saw Red Willow on foot running. He called to me:
"Cousin, my horse is killed!" So I caught up a sol-
dier's horse that was dragging a rope and brought it
to Red Willow while the soldiers were shooting fast
at me. Just then, for a little while, I was a wanekia[3]
myself. In this fight Long Bear and another man,
whose name I have forgotten, were badly wounded;
but we saved them and carried them along with us.
The soldiers did not follow us far into the Badlands,
and when it was night we rode back with our
wounded to the O-ona-gazhee.

We wanted a much bigger war-party so that we
could meet the soldiers and get revenge. But this
was hard, because the people were not all of the
same mind, and they were hungry and cold. We had
a meeting there, and were all ready to go out with
more warriors, when Afraid-of-His-Horses came over
from Pine Ridge to make peace with Red Cloud,
who was with us there.

Our party wanted to go out and fight anyway, but
Red Cloud made a speech to us something like this:
"Brothers, this is a very hard winter. The women
and children are starving and freezing. If this were
summer, I would say to keep on fighting to the end.
But we cannot do this. We must think of the wom-
en and children and that it is very bad for them. So
we must make peace, and I will see that nobody is
hurt by the soldiers."

The people agreed to this, for it was true. So we
broke camp next day and went down from the O-ona-
gazhee to Pine Ridge, and many, many Lakotas
were already there. Also, there were many, many
soldiers. They stood in two lines with their guns held

[3] A "make-live," savior.

in front of them as we went through to where we camped.

And so it was all over.

I did not know then how much was ended. When I look back now from this high hill of my old age, I can still see the butchered women and children lying heaped and scattered all along the crooked gulch as plain as when I saw them with eyes still young. And I can see that something else died there in the bloody mud, and was buried in the blizzard. A people's dream died there. It was a beautiful dream.

And I, to whom so great a vision was given in my youth,—you see me now a pitiful old man who has done nothing, for the nation's hoop is broken and scattered. There is no center any longer, and the sacred tree is dead.

Author's Postscript

After the conclusion of the narrative, Black Elk and our party were sitting at the north edge of Cuny Table, looking off across the Badlands ("the beauty and the strangeness of the earth," as the old man expressed it). Pointing at Harney Peak that loomed black above the far sky-rim, Black Elk said: "There, when I was young, the spirits took me in my vision to the center of the earth and showed me all the good things in the sacred hoop of the world. I wish I could stand up there in the flesh before I die, for there is something I want to say to the Six Grandfathers."

So the trip to Harney Peak was arranged, and a few days later we were there. On the way up to the summit, Black Elk remarked to his son, Ben: "Something should happen to-day. If I have any power left, the thunder beings of the west should hear me when I send a voice, and there should be at least a little thunder and a little rain." What happened is, of course, related to Wasichu readers as being merely a more or less striking coincidence. It was a bright and cloudless day, and after we had

reached the summit the sky was perfectly clear. It was a season of drouth, one of the worst in the memory of the old men. The sky remained clear until about the conclusion of the ceremony.

"Right over there," said Black Elk, indicating a point of rock, "is where I stood in my vision, but the hoop of the world about me was different, for what I saw was in the spirit."

Having dressed and painted himself as he was in his great vision, he faced the west, holding the sacred pipe before him in his right hand. Then he sent forth a voice; and a thin, pathetic voice it seemed in that vast space around us:

'Hey-a-a-hey! Hey-a-a-hey! Hey-a-a-hey! Hey-a-a-hey! Grandfather, Great Spirit, once more behold me on earth and lean to hear my feeble voice. You lived first, and you are older than all need, older than all prayer. All things belong to you—the two-leggeds, the four-leggeds, the wings of the air and all green things that live. You have set the powers of the four quarters to cross each other. The good road and the road of difficulties you have made to cross; and where they cross, the place is holy. Day in and day out, forever, you are the life of things.

"Therefore I am sending a voice, Great Spirit, my Grandfather, forgetting nothing you have made, the stars of the universe and the grasses of the earth.

"You have said to me, when I was still young and could hope, that in difficulty I should send a voice four times, once for each quarter of the earth, and you would hear me.

"To-day I send a voice for a people in despair.

"You have given me a sacred pipe, and through this I should make my offering. You see it now.

"From the west, you have given me the cup of

232

living water and the sacred bow, the power to make live and to destroy. You have given me a sacred wind and the herb from where the white giant lives —the cleansing power and the healing. The daybreak star and the pipe, you have given from the east; and from the south, the nation's sacred hoop and the tree that was to bloom. To the center of the world you have taken me and showed the goodness and the beauty and the strangeness of the greening earth, the only mother—and there the spirit shapes of things, as they should be, you have shown to me and I have seen. At the center of this sacred hoop you have said that I should make the tree to bloom.

"With tears running, O Great Spirit, Great Spirit, my Grandfather—with running tears I must say now that the tree has never bloomed. A pitiful old man, you see me here, and I have fallen away and have done nothing. Here at the center of the world, where you took me when I was young and taught me; here, old, I stand, and the tree is withered, Grandfather, my Grandfather!

"Again, and maybe the last time on this earth, I recall the great vision you sent me. It may be that some little root of the sacred tree still lives. Nourish it then, that it may leaf and bloom and fill with singing birds. Hear me, not for myself, but for my people; I am old. Hear me that they may once more go back into the sacred hoop and find the good red road, the shielding tree!"

We who listened now noted that thin clouds had gathered about us. A scant chill rain began to fall and there was low, muttering thunder without lightning. With tears running down his cheeks, the old man raised his voice to a thin high wail, and chanted: "In sorrow I am sending a feeble voice,

233

POSTSCRIPT

O Six Powers of the World. Hear me in my sorrow, for I may never call again. O make my people live!"

For some minutes the old man stood silent, with face uplifted, weeping in the drizzling rain.

In a little while the sky was clear again.

THE END

About This Book and Its Author

BLACK ELK SPEAKS is a book about a vision—a vision of spiritual values experienced by an aged Sioux medicine man during the Indians' great time of trouble. The concepts are revolutionary, as have been the visions of most seers, revolutionary not in economics or politics but in the universal concept of what life is all about. It is a holy man's revelation of the *quo vadis* that all men ask of themselves and of their fellowmen.

Black Elk's vision recognizes neither race nor creed nor geography. It is as universal as the teachings of Buddha or Christ or Mohammed or Marcus Aurelius or St. Thomas Aquinas or St. Francis of Assisi or Thoreau or Emerson. The universality of *Black Elk Speaks* is evidenced by its having been already translated into eight foreign languages: German, Flemish, Dutch, Italian, Danish, Serbo-Croatian, Swedish, and Spanish.

Black Elk was an illiterate and spoke no English. He was an ancient, waiting out his last days on the Pine Ridge Reservation, hoping only that he might "save his great vision for men." In John G. Neihardt,

epic and lyric poet and familiar with Indians for many years, Black Elk found the man who could understand and interpret and give form to the message.

Neihardt was led to Black Elk some forty years ago while working on his *The Song of the Messiah,* one of his two *Twilight of the Sioux* epic songs. *The Song of the Messiah* tells of the Messiah Movement that arose among the Plains Indians in the 1880s, when they had sunk into the depths of desperation under the genocidal assault of the white man. Neihardt knew Black Elk to be a holy man who had been of some importance in the Messiah Movement and who was a second cousin to Crazy Horse, leader of the Sioux in the Indian Wars. Black Elk had refused to relate his vision to other whites; he accepted Neihardt immediately with the words: "He has been sent to learn what I know, and I will teach him."

Black Elk's personal story, spoken in Sioux and translated by his son, was not a chronological, cohesive, organized account of his life and vision. It was, rather, a series of reminiscences of incidents and events, and of flashbacks of memory. Often Black Elk's narrative was supplemented by the recollections of his old friends, who also had lived through the time of troubles.

Black Elk Speaks is actually a re-creation in English of the holy man's account of his life and vision, given form, coherence, and chronology by Neihardt. With his deep insight into, and knowledge of, Sioux mysticism, Neihardt was well chosen as go-between for the wise old medicine man and those to whom he hoped to communicate his message.

An adopted member of the Oglala Sioux, chosen by Black Elk as heir to the seer's mystic powers,

Neihardt has, in addition to writing *Black Elk Speaks,* told the story of the Sioux in prose and epic.

Born near Sharpsburg, Illinois, January 8, 1881, third child of Nicholas Nathan Neihardt and Alice Culler Neihardt, John G. Neihardt and his mother and two sisters went to live with his pioneer grandparents in a sod house on the upper Solomon River in Kansas in 1886. Two years later they moved to Kansas City, and from there, in 1891, to Wayne, Nebraska. There he attended the pioneer Nebraska Normal College, graduating with a B.S. degree at the age of sixteen.

His first book, *The Divine Enchantment,* a long poem based on the Vedanta philosophy, was finished when he was sixteen and published when he was nineteen.

After teaching at a country school for two terms, he moved to Bancroft, Nebraska, where he worked with an Indian trader among the Omahas. Later he edited a country weekly, the *Bancroft Blade,* for several years. Thereafter he devoted his time to the writing of fiction and lyric verse with rapidly increasing national success. During this period he lived much among the Omaha Indians, becoming an authority on their traditions and customs.

He was married in 1908 to Mona Martinsen (1884–1958), sculptress and former student of Rodin. Their children are Enid, Sigurd, Hilda, and Alice.

In 1912, at the age of thirty-one, Neihardt began writing his major work, *A Cycle of the West,* composed of five epic songs "designed to celebrate the great mood of courage that was developed west of the Missouri River during that period which began in 1822 and ended in 1890": *The Song of Three*

Friends, The Song of Hugh Glass, The Song of Jed Smith, The Song of the Indian Wars, and *The Song of the Messiah.* Published individually as they were completed, they were issued in a single volume in 1949.

Recipient of numerous awards and honors, Neihardt holds honorary degrees from the University of Nebraska, Lincoln, Litt. D. (1917); Creighton University, Omaha, LL.D. (1935); and University of Missouri, Columbia, Litt. D. (1947). He is official Poet Laureate of the State of Nebraska, where a bronze bust of him executed by his wife has been placed in the rotunda of the Capitol. An annual state-wide Neihardt Day is observed at Bancroft, Nebraska, where his old study has been restored and a Sioux Prayer Garden has been constructed in his honor.

At ninety years of age, he still makes public appearances, reciting long passages from his epics and his lyrics by memory, for his sight is too poor to read print.